T0339515

Cambridge Elements ≡

Elements in Music since 1945
edited by
Mervyn Cooke
University of Nottingham

THEORY OF PROMINENCE

Temporal Structure of Music Based on Linguistic Stress

Bryan Hayslett
New World School of the Arts

CAMBRIDGE
UNIVERSITY PRESS

CAMBRIDGE
UNIVERSITY PRESS

University Printing House, Cambridge CB2 8BS, United Kingdom

One Liberty Plaza, 20th Floor, New York, NY 10006, USA

477 Williamstown Road, Port Melbourne, VIC 3207, Australia

314–321, 3rd Floor, Plot 3, Splendor Forum, Jasola District Centre,
New Delhi – 110025, India

103 Penang Road, #05–06/07, Visioncrest Commercial, Singapore 238467

Cambridge University Press is part of the University of Cambridge.

It furthers the University's mission by disseminating knowledge in the pursuit of
education, learning, and research at the highest international levels of excellence.

www.cambridge.org
Information on this title: www.cambridge.org/9781108813334
DOI: 10.1017/9781108884402

First published 2022

A catalogue record for this publication is available from the British Library.

ISBN 978-1-108-81333-4 Paperback
ISSN 2632-7791 (online)
ISSN 2632-7783 (print)

Theory of Prominence

Temporal Structure of Music Based on Linguistic Stress

Elements in Music since 1945

DOI: 10.1017/9781108884402
First published online: July 2022

Bryan Hayslett
New World School of the Arts

Author for correspondence: Bryan Hayslett, HayslettCello@gmail.com

Abstract: Many twentieth- and twenty-first-century composers have written music with rhythmic structures that must be understood through a framework distinct from even periodic meter, which has been a salient musical feature of Western classical music for centuries. This Element's analytical system outlines structure and phrasing in sections of music without even perceptible meter. Instead of entrainment to meter, Bryan Hayslett theorizes that listeners perceive rhythm in similar ways to how they perceive the rhythm of language. With gesture as the smallest organizational grouping unit, his analytical system combines Fred Lerdahl and Ray Jackendoff's generative theory of tonal music with Bruce Hayes's metrical stress theory from linguistics. The listener perceives the shape of a gesture according to the structure of its constituents, and larger-level phrasing is perceived through the hierarchical relationship of gestures. After developing a set of rules, the author provides analyses that outline temporal structure according to perceptual prominence.

Keywords: linguistics, phrasing, music theory, performance, music and language

ISBNs: 9781108813334 (PB), 9781108884402 (OC)
ISSNs: 2632-7791 (online), 2632-7783 (print)

Contents

1 Tales of a Cellist   1

2 On Prominence: Language and Music   5

3 Rules for Analysis   8

4 Analyses   31

5 Conclusion   68

References   70

1 Tales of a Cellist

Throughout my journey learning to play the cello, I have sought to describe my repertoire in the most personal ways possible, in order to connect more deeply with the music and therefore perform the pieces more convincingly. However, as I explored more recently written works outside of the "standard" repertoire, I encountered phrase structures that I did not understand how to shape effectively and established forms of analysis offered little aid. My teachers' suggestions included exacerbating the dynamics, thinking of lines as gestures, and focusing on tone color. Although these ideas helped tremendously, I sought a more systematic and quantifiable way to describe phrasing. As an educator, what would I tell my students to help them understand and perform such music? Performing Baroque, classical, or romantic music without an understanding of the meter seems absurd, yet little exists to explain the temporal structures that operate outside of conventional meter.

I was invigorated to develop an analytical framework upon hearing the music of Lee Hyla (1952–2014), a composer born in the United States of America and active in New York City, Boston, and Chicago. I was immediately struck by the energy and intensity in his works, particularly in sections in which I could not hear a steady pulse, and had strong emotional reactions to his music despite not immediately understanding how it worked. I was most taken by Hyla's *Dream of Innocent III* (*DOI3*) (1987) for amplified cello, piano, and percussion, which underscores formal divisions with differing temporal aesthetics. The score further piqued my interest with markings such as *fast and brutal* (m. 16), Rocking (m. 120), and Wild and Impassioned (m. 206). Although much of the piece is structured upon a steady beat, I noticed that many of my favorite sections were written with complex changing meters. I felt the rhythms in Hyla's music were a significant component and later learned that Hyla's sense of rhythm was imbued with influence from Elliott Carter as well as nonclassical artists including James Brown (funk), Neil Young (singer/songwriter), Captain Beefheart (avant-garde rock), and Cecil Taylor (free jazz piano). These artists were outliers in their own genres, and rhythm is a salient feature of all of their music. Hyla's complex rhythms felt grounded despite a lack of a steady underlying pulse. This temporal aesthetic is not unique to his music, but little research exists to meaningfully describe structure in music without isochronous meter.

I believed if I addressed how I was perceiving the music, then I would be able to phrase it in a way that felt natural to the listener. To me, the melodic lines sounded like an instrumental version of speech, and I began to explore how an understanding of linguistics could relate to the performance and perception of contemporary music without an isochronous beat. I began my investigation with Fred Lerdahl and Ray Jackendoff's *Generative Theory of Tonal Music* (GTTM) because it is reflective of principles in universal psychological processes that inform musical analysis (Lerdahl & Jackendoff 1983). Although GTTM addresses the perception of rhythm and time through generative models borrowed from linguistics, the theory applies to tonal music and does not address much of the music being written today.

Without a meaningful rhythmic analysis from GTTM, I turned to linguistics, which explains the experience of rhythm according to perceptual salience because spoken syllables do not align with an even metrical grid and do not have even rhythms. Specifically, I am referring to metrical stress theory, which was first formalized in 1977 by Mark Liberman and Alan Prince, expanded in Morris Halle and Jean-Roger Vergnaud's *An Essay on Stress* (1987), and further codified by Bruce Hayes in his 1995 book. Hayes's book describes rhythm and emphasis in language as the culmination of his work in phonology regarding linguistic stress and metrical structure. I theorize that listeners experience rhythm in music without a steady pulse in the same way that they experience the rhythm of speech. Although stress theory was codified in English, the theory applies to many languages that organize according to stress; Hayes's analyses include examples from numerous languages.[1] The structures elucidated by his theory do not apply only to English speakers.

My analyses outline structure and phrasing in music without periodic meter to aid performers.[2] I developed this theory through careful study of late twentieth-century music written in the United States of America, but I believe the result to be more widely applicable. My theory is an extension of GTTM with Hayes's stress theory, and I present my final analyses in the form of tree structures that indicate the hierarchy of perceptual prominence within an excerpt.

1.1 General Structure

I must note three foci in discussing perception: the notated score, the performer's mental construction, and the listener's perception, the last of which is the focus of my analyses. The score is an intermediary device between the conception and the realization of a piece, so the notated meters do not necessarily relate to how the listener hears the music. This suggests the listener experiences two

---

[1] A representative list: Arabic, Cahuilla, Wargamay, Maithili, Hindi, Lenakel, Auca, Icelandic, Hixkaryana, Choctaw, Chickasaw, Creek, Seminole, Winnebago, Cayuga, Pacific Yupik, and Asheninca, among others.

[2] Unlike the repertoire discussed in Fred Lerdahl's (1992) seminal work "Cognitive Constraints on Compositional Systems," I discuss music that is cognitively accessible.

simultaneous structures: one created by the meter and another arising from the organization of prominent events on the musical surface. These two structures are often aligned in older repertoire, but temporal interest in metrical music is created through the misalignment of the meter and prominent events on the musical surface. However, periodic meter eclipses the prominence structure, which is only described in relation to the meter rather than recognized as an independent entity. For instance, syncopation and hemiola are two types of misalignment between these structures, but neither are disorienting for the listener because the prominent events are understood in relation to the regularity of the metrical structure. In music without a periodic meter, the listener must attend to the structure suggested by the events themselves rather than placing the rhythms in relation to an underlying meter; my analyses seek to foreground and describe this prominence structure. I do not seek to summon structures that were previously nonexistent, but rather to elucidate the prominence structure that is almost entirely overshadowed when periodic meter is present. In contemporary music without periodic meter, phrasing must thus rely entirely on the prominence structure.

To relate phrasing to temporal structures, my analytical approach extends GTTM with Hayes's stress theory as a guiding principle, to focus on perceptual models that unite music and language. GTTM contains four components: grouping structure, metrical structure, time-span reduction, and prolongational reduction. However, I only address grouping and metrical structures; time-span and prolongational reductions rely on the same structures but focus on harmonic information, which is not the goal of my analyses.

Although my methodology involves linguistics, my analyses here do not include repertoire that involves speaking or singing. My focus is on deeper experiential connections between language and music, and works including conscious rhythmic connections between the two domains present a different analytical interest. In such pieces, the music is explicitly affected by language, whereas my work explores underlying connections between music and language.

Although my analyses rely on rhythm as a central factor, I address pitch and harmony tangentially as they relate to perceptual prominence. My analyses highlight perceptible structures related to phrasing by focusing on the salience of rhythm and meter as organizing principles. Although I involve elements of pitch in my analyses, I do not attempt to codify harmonic structure in the works from which I draw the musical examples. My theory applies to the phrase level of a piece and does not extend to higher hierarchical levels, such as the perceived salience of events within sections of an entire piece.

GTTM, the foundation of my theory, was co-authored by composer Lerdahl and linguist Jackendoff, who is also a clarinetist. The theory described perception of musical structures inspired by Noam Chomsky's generative linguistic theory (Chomsky 1957, 1965, 1968). GTTM was grounded in the authors' musical intuitions of heard structure in tonal music, and many of its principles have been successfully tested empirically.[3] In order to describe analogous heard constructions in post-tonal music, I extend the theory with linguistic ideas associated with Hayes's metrical stress theory.

GTTM assumes a regular periodic meter and a recurring beat hierarchy in each measure, so temporal tension must be described differently without these two conditions. Employing another linguistic theory to describe emphasis in post-tonal music aligns with the theory's origins. As linguistic stress is hierarchical without evenness, the concept is useful when analyzing music without a constant, evenly spaced beat. Metrical stress theory suggests stress in language manifests as linguistic rhythm. Examining rhythm, meter, and temporality in a post-tonal context using widely accepted perspectives from linguistics contributes to an understanding of phrasing, in terms of both interpretation and perception, and provides a framework within which to comprehend structure.

Extending GTTM with constructs from language does not distort it, as the theory itself is deeply indebted to linguistic theory. My analyses are based on the points in time that draw the listener's focus as based on emphasis in lieu of an underlying metrical structure as a grounding force. Events with greater perceptual salience are acknowledged as receiving greater emphasis within the prominence hierarchy. The emphasis that signals perceptual salience is more than just phenomenal accent, and I analyze music according to perceptual systems that structure stress in language.

Stress translates to music because the concept is not unique to language; it is a perceptual rather than physical phenomenon. Lerdahl mentions that stress is an important marker in both language and music because the perception of both syllables and pitch events "is one of relative sonic prominence within its immediate context" (Lerdahl 2001: 339). In both domains, no single physical correlate directly reflects stress or emphasis; the concept "unifies in a coherent way a broad set of phenomena" (Hayes 1995: 9). The perceptual markers of stress, in order of saliency, are pitch contour, duration, and loudness, the last of which is relatively unimportant (Fry 1955, 1958). Specific characteristics of contour, duration, and loudness do not invariably signal stress; for example, high pitches do not always signal stress. In English, pitch is one of the most

---

[3] See Deliège 1987; Palmer & Krumhansl 1987, 1990; Bigand & Pineau 1997; Large & Palmer 2002; Peretz & Coltheart 2003; Frankland et al. 2004; Lalitte et al. 2009; Koelsch et al. 2013.

powerful cues for stress, but the lowest pitch in the intonational contour of yes/ no questions is the most stressed, whereas higher pitches are correlated with stress in other contexts. Lerdahl and Jackendoff define local stress as accent or "extra intensity on the attack of a pitch-event," citing several forms of notated accents (Lerdahl & Jackendoff 1983: 78). Stress is not dependent on the specific linguistic structures of words and syllables because rhythms can be detected in many formats such as steps on pavement, machinery in motion, musical notes, or speech. Also, stress outlines a temporal structure that does not assume evenness or periodicity.

The primary goal of my research is to discuss temporal tension in music without an even beat, exploring how linguistic stress contributes to the analysis of recently written works. I focus on perceptible structures in order to relate the listener's hearing of the music to practical performance applications.

2 On Prominence: Language and Music

Studies have shown a relationship between the rhythm of a composer's language and their music by comparing the durational variability of each.[4] For instance, a sequence of quarter notes with one eighth note will have very little durational variability as compared to a combination of notes of different durational values. Languages work similarly; each language is referred to as rhythmically organized around either stress or syllables. Stress-timed languages, such as English, German, Russian, and Arabic, organize around stresses, in that syllables vary greatly in length. For example, each word in the sentence "cats chase birds" includes a perceptual focus and relative rhythmic evenness that persists even when expanding the sentence with more words, such as "the cats are chasing the birds"; the added words are spoken with much shorter syllables. Syllable-timed languages, such as French, Italian, Finnish, and Turkish, are spoken with each syllable lasting roughly the same amount of time. Different amounts of durational variability can be measured with the normalized pairwise variability index (nPVI). This metric measures durational variability in sequences of attack points and has traditionally been applied to language. However, the nPVI can also measure durational variability in music.

Aniruddh Patel and Joseph Daniele showed a link between language and musical rhythm by examining works by English and French composers. English is stress-timed, and French is syllable-timed; this is reflected in the nPVI because English speech has a higher durational variability than French. This relationship is also reflected in English and French music, as shown in Ex. 1. Patel and Daniele drew source material from the Barlow and Morgenstern's

---

[4] See Huron & Ollen 2003; Patel & Daniele 2003a, 2003b; Daniele & Patel 2013.

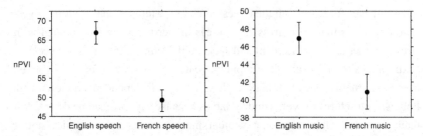

Example 1 Proportional relationship of English and French speech and music[5]

Dictionary of Musical Themes (1983), choosing composers born in the nineteenth century who died in the twentieth century, native speakers of either British English or French who lived and worked in their respective countries. Each composer had to have at least five qualifying themes. Themes were excluded that referenced song or had external rhythmic or stylistic intentions, such as stylized dances or music replicating that of another culture. This comparison was successfully replicated with more composers and languages by David Huron and Joy Ollen, to show that the rhythmic variability of composers' native languages affects their use of musical rhythm (Huron & Ollen 2003).

These qualities inform my examination of music with uneven rhythmic values and infrequent or varied repetition. Speech breaks down by group into sentences, phrases, and words, which can be understood as analogous to musical phrases and gestures. Because the rhythm of English speech is organized around stresses, syllables vary greatly in length. Curated speech, such as poetry or prepared speech, is often presented with a consciously controlled rhythm, but I am focusing on the rhythm of unplanned speaking.

Words in language and pitch in music can obscure the temporal similarities, but the speech-like quality of rhythms is perceptible through an aural comparison. To show the similarities, the following discussion juxtaposes examples of English speech and an excerpt from one of Hyla's piano trios. I highlight the rhythm of the following examples by removing words and pitches, reducing each syllable and note to a single click. Because I have not located a recording of Hyla speaking, I am using my own speech as I am a native English speaker with a geographic trajectory similar to Hyla's. Audio Example 1 contains audio of my reading aloud the first sentence of this paragraph. The sentence groups into small fragments, like gestures, and two main sections, like sub-phrases.

---

[5] Reproduced from Patel & Daniele 2003a: B38, B41.

Audio Example 1 Hayslett speech

The following excerpt from the middle of Hyla's piano trio *Amnesia Redux* (2002) shows the similarity of Hyla's rhythms to speech. The music in AEx. 2 can be heard as small gestures that relate more closely to speech than to tonal music, in terms of rhythm.

Audio Example 2 Hyla *Amnesia Redux* excerpt

This speech-like quality of rhythm is often disguised by pitch and harmony, so the following two audio examples present these excerpts reduced to rhythm alone. Changes in pitch are not salient to the listener's segmentation of the musical surface, so temporal structure is an important factor in analyzing perception and affect (Lalitte et al. 2009).

The similarity between Hyla's rhythms and speech rhythms is an important link to investigate because it is a factor that affects the aesthetic of the music, and the following audio examples show the similarity between the rhythms by removing everything except the rhythm. Each tick represents a syllable in AEx. 3 and the inception of a note in AEx. 4.

Audio Example 3 Hayslett speech reduced to rhythm[6]

Audio Example 4 Hyla *Amnesia Redux* excerpt, reduced to rhythm

---

[6] I created AEX. 3 and AEX. 4 manually using Garageband.

Through these examples, I have shown similarity between the rhythms in English speech and in Hyla's music, which exemplifies a connection between rhythm in language and rhythm in music without a periodic beat. Jackendoff summarizes the connection between musical and linguistic rhythm, writing that "the similarities between musical rhythm and linguistic prosody are striking – although neither is reducible to the other. The two are related more or less like fingers and toes" (Jackendoff 2003: 80). Research has proven a subconscious link between temporality in composers' music and their native languages, and this motivated the use of linguistic theory in the creation of my framework. Whether or not composers consciously use speech-like rhythms, linguistics provides a useful perspective in analyzing the resulting constructions.

3 Rules for Analysis

Rhythmic vocabulary is part and parcel of musical discussions, but I here define a few important terms used in my analyses. *Pulse* refers to a sequence of perceptually prominent points in time. The beats within the pulse are typically evenly spaced, but they do not have to be as long as they follow a pattern. Rhythms occur in relationship to the pulse, which is maintained internally by the performer and can be perceived by the listener. A pulse theoretically exists at all hierarchical levels, but I discuss the term in reference to the tactus, or the level of the temporal hierarchy to which listeners most often tap. If the pulse is "temporally regular," listeners are able to anticipate future beats (London 2012: 9). In tonal music with an evenly spaced tactus, the pulse is often a shared perception between the listener and the performer; this evenness is a salient structural factor of the tonal tradition. The pulse could also be uneven as long as it exists within a recurring pattern, such as a beat pattern of 3+3+2 often heard in rock music. The hierarchical level of pulse to which the majority of listeners would tap their feet or nod their heads is reffered to as the *tactus* level; this varies widely between pieces of music.

When the tactus level is not evenly spaced in time or does not contain a regular pattern, the concept of pulse diverges into separate experiences for the performer and listener. The performer maintains an internal sense of time mimicking an uneven pulse that matches the notated music, thereby sustaining tempo and placing rhythms; the beats maintained by the performer are in accordance with the metrical organization of the piece whether or not the beats are evenly spaced. The listener does not perceive pulse if the music lacks temporal regularity or a pattern; points of perceptual emphasis replace the listener's sense of pulse in these situations. Analytically, prominence structure replaces metrical structure.

Meter is notated on the musical surface as measures. In tonal music, measures typically contain the same number of evenly spaced beats throughout one piece or movement. Meter is "the anticipatory schema that is the result of our inherent abilities to entrain to periodic stimuli in our environment" (London 2012: 12), analogous to a "yardstick whereby we locate the musical events of the piece in a grid of time-points" (Lester 1986: 118). This grouping of the pulse allows for hierarchical metrical structure, but perception of meter changes without periodicity just as with pulse. The performer maintains a sense of the notated meter, but the listener is likely unaware of its exact delineations. In much contemporary music, including the excerpts I will analyze, meter is a notational tool to provide a temporal grid and communicate local structure; it is not intended to be a perceptual phenomenon for the audience.

Isochronous meter is structured with beats at the tactus level that recur at evenly spaced points in time, usually in measures with the same recurring time signature. However, isochronous meter can exist between measures that can all be divided evenly by the tactus pulse, such as 3/4 and 4/4 that can be divided into quarter notes. In actual performance, meter is hardly ever isochronous due to slight deviations.

3.1 The Experienced Listener

In tonal music, temporal structure relies heavily on a perceptible meter. Through this device, listeners anticipate future beats and relate surface rhythms to an underlying regularity. However, in music lacking rhythmic evenness and meter as an experienced structure, the perceptually prominent beats in the heard structure must be analyzed without a sense of entrainment to meter; prominence emerges as an independent framework. To address temporal structure within these sections of music, my analyses outline underlying structures and aid with phrasing. Perceiving rhythmic and temporal structure in both music and language involves related processes.

Lerdahl and Jackendoff suggest that "a piece of music is a mentally constructed entity" and that the goal of music theory should be "to explicate this mentally produced organization" (Lerdahl & Jackendoff 1983: 2). The listener's musical intuitions and perception create the heard structure, a phenomenon that requires experience with the musical idiom in order to organize the sounds meaningfully, according to GTTM. The theory addresses the listener's final mental construction of a piece rather than real-time processing while listening. Rules assign analyses to pieces rather than leaving it to the analyst to fit the theoretical specifics to a piece, but the rules are meant to allow an understanding of the value of different readings of a work; no two listeners will hear a piece of music in the same way. Although Lerdahl and Jackendoff use the concept of an experienced listener, they acknowledge certain universal principles of musical grammar. Ultimately, their assessment of the success of GTTM is contingent upon the information it reveals about a specific piece, how it addresses the nature of tonal music and music in general, and how it relates to cognitive theory in a broader sense (Lerdahl & Jackendoff 1983: 4).

With inspiration from Chomsky, the theory is "based in part on the goals and methodology, but not the substance, of generative linguistics" (Lerdahl & Jackendoff 1983: 45). Generative linguistic theory characterizes people's linguistic knowledge while speaking a language they know. Humans can understand and construct an infinite number of unique sentences without ever hearing them before, which involves an understanding beyond knowledge acquired through direct instruction alone. Similarly, people can process and relate to music they have never heard before. Many other parallels have been made between music and language, but GTTM focuses on this cognitive capacity.

A GTTM analysis compares the coherence of different possible perceptions of a piece to determine which are the more or less preferred interpretations or the structures that the idealized "experienced listener" would more or less likely attribute to the music (Lerdahl & Jackendoff 1983: 9). The theory contains structures based on *well-formedness rules* (WFRs) that provide the conditions for all possible analyses and *preference rules* (PRs) that suggest which of the possible analyses more closely match the heard structure. The two aspects of GTTM pertinent to the development of my methodology are grouping structure and metrical structure, each of which has its own set of WFRs and PRs. However, the process is not an automated, straightforward assignment of an analysis because pieces invariably present conflicts between the rules. Broader context and relationships guide the prioritization of different rules in each situation. In this way, each analysis reflects some degree of interpretation, but my approach is also based on rules to describe structures within the music.

The primary component of GTTM that I employ is grouping structure, about which the authors write that "the rules for grouping seem to be idiom-independent – that is, a listener needs to know relatively little about a musical idiom in order to assign grouping structure to pieces in that idiom" (Lerdahl & Jackendoff 1983: 36). Irène Deliège proved that the rules for grouping structure apply broadly between musicians and nonmusicians alike (Deliège 1987: 356). Lerdahl and Jackendoff also recognize grouping structure as one of the most important factors that performers can manipulate to project their "(largely unconscious) preferred analysis" of the pieces they perform (Lerdahl & Jackendoff 1983: 63–64). Because grouping allows for interpretive decisions by performers and is a structure perceptible to listeners without idiomatic knowledge of music, the concept is essential to laying out musical phrasing, and performers must be aware of how their articulation and breathing will affect the heard structure.

With regard to temporal structures, I relate the concept of "experience" to linguistic knowledge. Rhythmically speaking, knowledge of language is analogous to the idiom that experienced listeners have encountered. Every language operates with stress, although the specific patterns differ between languages. I theorize that the way speakers of stress-timed languages grasp linguistic rhythm reflects principles of perception that apply to the heard structure of music, regardless of the language spoken by the listener. My analyses provide a layout for performers at the phrase level based on a hierarchy of perceptual prominence, evoking a hierarchical temporal structure other than meter.

Whereas grouping structure applies to music universally, GTTM's metrical structure relies on idiomatic knowledge. To account for other idioms, Lerdahl and Jackendoff mention the possibility of modifying or dropping metrical well-formedness rules (MWFRs) 3 and 4 because those are the rules that are idiom-specific (Lerdahl & Jackendoff 1983: 97). The metrical preference rules (MPRs) would also change drastically to describe music outside the tonal idiom, but altering the MWFRs suggests a fundamentally different construction of music. My framework relies on grouping structure, but stress theory guides the analysis of perceptually prominent time points in lieu of GTTM's metrical structure. Lerdahl and Jackendoff cite stress and length as "markers of metrical strength in music as well as in language," supporting stress as a device for temporal organization (Lerdahl & Jackendoff 1983: 85). Citing stress directly, MPR 4 suggests that stressed beats are preferably structured as strong beats, but I prioritize the concept and address it within grouping structure.

The goal of these rules, and my analyses, is to define the *heard structure*: the listener's cognition of a piece of music constructed from aural perception. The concept relates to cognitive psychology, specifically that "theoretical descriptions of musical patterns might offer suggestions about listeners' knowledge of music (sometimes referred to as schemas or mental representations). This knowledge presumably affects how music is encoded in perception, interpreted, remembered, and performed" (Krumhansl 1995: 54). The heard structure results from listeners organizing what they hear, "beyond the simple registering of such surface features as pitch, duration, volume, attack envelope, and timbre"; the organization is "distinct from anything the listener has been taught formally," so these structures operate outside of musical training (Jackendoff & Lerdahl 1981: 45).

3.2 Gesture

At the foundation of my grouping structure is gesture, which is fundamental to understanding structure in music without evenness, but the term "gesture" carries a wide range of definitions and connotations. Most commonly, the discussion of gesture begins with physical movement, and the structure of musical gestures is understood to rely on physicality (Godøy & Leman 2009). Such physical motions are intended to communicate information and feeling, ranging from some gestures that are innately understood (Trevarthen et al. 2011: 21) to others that have evolved dependent upon the meaning within the "social interactive context" (McNeill 2000: 12). For instance, a smile might be widely recognized as a signal of happiness or approval, whereas a rude gesture in one country would be meaningless to someone unfamiliar with that culture. A sense of gesture is fundamental to the human experience and to interaction between people, seen ubiquitously in communication between people who do not speak a common language; in an effort to be understood, words are replaced by physical motions, such as pointing at subway stops on maps, and varying the speed of movement suggests different affects. Gestures add information to words but can also function in place of them.

Robert Hatten has written extensively about perception and musical gesture in tonal music and distills the term to a basic human competency not unique to music: "the ability to recognize the significance of energetic shaping through time" (Hatten 2004: 93). Hatten's theory is based in the tonal tradition, however, which emphasizes symmetry and evenness. According to Justin London, humans not only respond to regularities in the environment but also project regularity and order onto stimuli (London 2012: 13). Gestures in music without even meter rarely display regularity, and listeners cannot project temporal order in these situations; as such, the listener relies heavily on the performer's phrasing to experience organization. The structure of gestures is vital to describing perception because they provide a map of salient events in lieu of regularity; some events are more salient than others.[7] The listener does not attend to every note within a gesture equally, and the perceptual foci can be delineated through stress theory from linguistics. The hierarchy of gestures therefore lays out underlying structures independent of evenness or symmetry. The listener perceives the shape of each gesture according to the structure of its constituents, and larger-level phrasing is perceived through the hierarchical relationship of gestures.

Hatten articulates a fundamental link between speech and gesture: "the prototypical musical gesture is a unit in the perceptual present (typically within two seconds). It has initiation and closure, such that we can speak of a series of gestures, or gestural units. These units are analogous to prosodic units in speech, organized around nuclear points of emphasis, or beats" (Hatten 2004: 94).

---

[7] In ecological psychology, James Gibson uses the term *economical perception* to suggest that listeners attend selectively to the information needed rather than attending to all of the information available (Gibson 1966).

Musical gestures are not identical to groups as defined by GTTM because gestures are shaped with points of emphasis. For instance, nodding my head at different speeds will communicate different intentions. This is a challenging concept to attempt to define in music because the listener experiences a multitude of parameters that can gradually change including dynamics, tempo, articulation, and tone color, all of which are controlled and shaped by the performer gradually changing the amount of energy they use; listeners can experience relative prominence of notes within a gesture according to the performer's use of energy. Extending upon the basis of Hatten's theory, I define the term *musical gesture* as a group of contiguous musical events with energetic shaping through time.

Although music lacks an analog to linguistic semantics, gestures communicate other information in music. Gesture is essential to aesthetic and represents a key aspect of communication with the audience. Performance is inherently gestural because sound is created on every instrument through some physical motion, but there is not always a connection between a musical gesture and the physical actions required to produce it (Zbikowski 2011: 83). For instance, the most salient notes receive their intensity from the construction of the music rather than from the amount of the performer's movement at that moment; the movement comes from the notes rather than the performing body. Musical gestures function aurally rather than kinesthetically and represent the synthesis of several technical aspects of sound. Interpretation of gestures depends on the context, just as physical gestures are affected by social norms (McNeill 2000: 11). In music without an even meter, gestures are the foundation of the hierarchy. Regardless of the tonality of the work, traditional analyses do not describe how gesture functions or how it relates to structure and phrasing. At the lowest level, the way a performer executes gestures will directly impact how the audience will aurally group the musical surface.

In lieu of an even, perceptible meter, temporal structure relies on the juxtaposition and relationship of each gesture. According to Joel Lester, "without the perceptual metric grid synchronized with the sounding music, the sense in which some events anticipate the beat, are suspended past the beat, or arrive on the beat is irrelevant" (Lester 1986: 122). Tension must be addressed in other terms. I theorize that temporal tension arises from the hierarchy of gestures rather than the conflict between rhythm and metrical beat.

3.3 Grouping Structure

The listener divides a piece of music into hierarchically related "motives, themes, phrases, periods, theme-groups, sections, and the piece itself," which

Example 2 Grouping 3/2 (shape)

Example 3 Grouping 3/2 reinforced

Example 4 Grouping 3/2 (pitch)

Example 5 Grouping 3/2 reinforced

is the aural representation of a common cognitive phenomenon (Lerdahl & Jackendoff 1983: 12). To illustrate a visual analog, the five items in Ex. 2 group according to shape as three circles and two squares. This is reinforced in Ex. 3 with the addition of a second factor, space. The same process occurs aurally as shown in Ex. 4 and Ex. 5.[8] The low notes represent circles; the high notes correspond to squares; and the quarter rest in Ex. 5 corresponds to the space.

The grouping well-formedness rules (GWFRs) delineate all possible constructions of groups, noting that a group must comprise adjacent notes ranging from a pair up to the size of an entire piece, and the hierarchy must be exhaustively partitioned with the entirety of each group belonging to the level above. Rests are not counted as events in grouping structure. The GWFRs on their own can create questionable structures, such as a 2/3 grouping in Ex. 3 or Ex. 5. Although these segmentations would be theoretically possible, they do not characterize the musical surface. The differing pitches and the rest would suggest a boundary to confirm a 3/2 grouping, which are characteristics involved in the grouping preference rules (GPRs) that guide decisions to match the music. GPRs delineate group boundaries based on note durations, symmetry, parallelism, and changes in register, dynamics, or articulation. Brackets above the staff enclose notes heard as belonging together at each hierarchical level.

---

[8] Examples 2–5 are inspired by Lerdahl & Jackendoff 1983: 41.

Example 6 Beethoven Cello Sonata No. 3, mm. 1–6: grouping structure

Example 6 shows the grouping structure of the opening of Beethoven's Sonata No. 3 for Cello and Piano, Op. 69. A grouping boundary exists after the third note because of the relatively long duration between attack points, as stated in GPR 2. The boundary in m. 4 is supported by GPR 6, the preference for parallelism with the beginning of the previous group, and by GPR 7 because it supports a more stable prolongational reduction, an aspect of GTTM involving harmony that does not apply to the development of my analyses. GPRs 2 and 7 also suggest a boundary after the E in m. 6, which is reinforced by a long separation between the inceptions of the E and the following note, making it a higher-level boundary.

GTTM's grouping structure translates to post-tonal music because the component reflects the auditory perception of rhythms irrespective of any rules of tonality. GPR 7 involves rules of harmonic reductions used in the latter part of GTTM, but the GWFRs and the other GPRs are integral to grouping in post-tonal music. While Ex. 6 is relatively straightforward, grouping structure in music without even meter can be considerably more opaque. Sometimes, several rules conflict; Ex. 7 presents a visual representation using shapes with an added element of color.[9] While the shapes suggest a 3/2 segmentation, the colors support a 2/3 grouping; either choice could be justified, so it depends on the larger context. Parallelism could aid in describing the structure, or perhaps one of the qualities takes priority throughout the work. Contextual information can usually be gleaned, illustrated in Ex. 8 and Ex. 9 as space. Visually, the space confirms the shape versus color decisions, but the space might represent a more subtle aspect in a piece of music. Prioritizing rules for such decisions is challenging due to the different contexts created by every composer and piece, but I attempt to provide a tool for examining these structures.

3.3.1 Grouping Structure Rules

I consider gesture as the smallest unit in grouping structure, most closely reminiscent of the foot in metrical stress theory. Feet most often comprise one or two syllables, but parsing music to single notes and pairs would be perceptually irrelevant. According to Hatten, the primary feature of a gesture involves

---

[9] Examples 7–9 are inspired by Lerdahl & Jackendoff 1983: 42.

Example 7 Conflicting grouping as either 3/2 (shape) or 2/3 (color)

Example 8 Grouping 3/2 (shape) reinforced by space

Example 9 Grouping 2/3 (color) reinforced by space

"energetic shaping through time," and I use the term to refer to small groups of notes that represent the lowest level of my framework (Hatten 2004: 93). The number of notes in each gesture varies according to context. For example, a set of eight notes would be parsed into gestures differently according to note values and tempo, with more notes in each gesture if thirty-second notes performed in a fast tempo and fewer if half notes performed in a slower tempo. GPR 1 suggests that very small groups are less preferable, so the fundamental structure of gesture must not be as limited as foot structure in linguistics. The primary principles that guide segmentation in language depend on grammatical and lexical rules, so my grouping component largely matches that of GTTM, with a few revisions.

The following discussion describes and outlines the GWFRs within my analytical framework. GWFR 1 states that groups comprise adjacent events. Listeners do not selectively group attack points separated by other events. This rule also allows for groups of any size, which is reinforced in GWFR 2.

GWFR 1 Any contiguous sequence of sound events can constitute a group, and only contiguous events can constitute a group

GWFR 2 clarifies that an entire piece is heard as a group rather than a sequence of unrelated events. Although my analyses describe structure only up to the phrase level, this rule remains unchanged from GTTM because I utilize grouping structure in a way that does not preclude the listener from perceiving larger scale grouping; however, prominence relationships at the level of an entire piece are likely undetectable.

GWFR 2 A piece constitutes a group.

The next rule describes the hierarchical nature of grouping structure. A group has the possibility of being segmented into smaller groups, although groups at the lowest level do not divide in any perceptually relevant ways.

GWFR 3 A group may contain smaller groups.

Grouping boundaries must be maintained throughout the hierarchy such that a boundary at one level exists at all smaller levels. This prevents a grouping analysis as shown in Ex. 10.

This rule would also preclude the grouping structure shown in Ex. 11. Overlapping and elided groups infrequently occur in tonal music, but the concepts are important to include. Post-tonal music often juxtaposes different musical material without transition, so the precise endings and beginnings of groups can be unclear. The techniques of overlap and elision serve the role of preventing a piece from coming to "a point of rhythmic completion," a technique that informs the aesthetic of much music without a perceptible meter (Lerdahl & Jackendoff 1983: 58). In the event of an overlap, expressed in my analyses as *(X)*, the event is simultaneously the end of a previous group and the beginning of the next group.

Overlaps occur when the final event of one group is also the first event of the following group. Elisions happen when the final event of one group is covered by a loud entrance of the next group on the same beat. In these cases, GTTM notes that the underlying structures must be well-formed, such that G_1 and G_2 in Ex. 11 must be well-formed groups on their own, before a listener perceives the shared event as an overlap or elision. I expand the following rule to recognize these special cases.

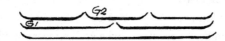

Example 10 Ill-formed boundary between levels[10]

Example 11 Overlapping grouping structure[11]

---

[10] Example reproduced from Lerdahl & Jackendoff 1983: 38.
[11] Example reproduced from Lerdahl & Jackendoff 1983: 38.

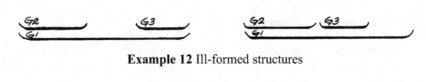

Example 12 Ill-formed structures

Example 13 Well-formed construction

GWFR 4 If a group G_1 contains part of a group G_2, it must contain all of G_2. In the case of overlaps and elisions, the underlying structures must be well-formed.

Further structuring the hierarchy, groups must be completely segmented. While GWFR 5 prevents constructions such as Ex. 12, this does not prevent constructions like Ex. 13 in which only part of the music is segmented at the lowest level.[12] Groups can be divided at lower hierarchical levels but must be exhaustively segmented at each level.

GWFR 5 If a group G_1 contains a smaller group G_2, then G_1 must be exhaustively partitioned into smaller groups.

The GWFRs designate possible constructions of groups, but all such possibilities of segmentation do not reflect the heard structure. To guide the placement of grouping boundaries, GPRs are based on perception and elucidate the conditions that suggest boundaries in the heard structure.

Having covered the rules for all possible grouping structures, I now hone in on the rules for the preferred structures. Gestures are the smallest grouping level of my analyses, which can vary widely in the number of events per gesture. GPR 1 supports that segmenting the music into groups of one or two notes, a literal transfer of stress theory, would not be well-formed. Although gestures are small groups, they must be large enough to be perceptually salient. There cannot be an exact limit to the number of events within a gesture because it depends heavily on tempo and note values.

GPR 1 Avoid analyses with very small groups – the smaller, the less preferable.

The proximity rule places boundaries according to temporal distance. Listeners segment at spaces between notes according to the distance between the end of one note and the beginning of the next and based on the time between attack points. This sense of distance depends on the immediate local context; the

---

[12] Examples reproduced from Lerdahl & Jackendoff 1983: 38–39.

distance of a quarter note would be relatively long in the middle of a passage of sixteenth notes and relatively short between whole notes.

GPR 2 (Proximity) Consider a sequence of four notes n_1 n_2 n_3 n_4. All else being equal, the transition $n_2 - n_3$ may be heard as a group boundary if

a. (Slur/Rest) the interval of time from the end of n_2 to the beginning of n_3 is greater than that from the end of n_1 to the beginning of n_2 and that from the end of n_3 to the beginning of n_4 or if
b. (Attack Point) the interval of time between the attack points of n_2 and n_3 is greater than that between the attack points of n_1 and n_2 and that between the attack points of n_3 and n_4.

GPR 3 suggests the heard structure relies on the perception of changes in the music. The rule focuses specifically on changes in register, dynamics, articulation, and note lengths. Similar to the previous rule, the strength of a change depends on the adjacent events for context.

GPR 3 (Change) Consider a sequence of four notes n_1 n_2 n_3 n_4. All else being equal, the transition $n_2 - n_3$ may be heard as a group boundary if

a. (Register) the transition $n_2 - n_3$ involves a greater intervallic distance than both $n_1 - n_2$ and $n_3 - n_4$ or if
b. (Dynamics) the transition $n_2 - n_3$ involves a change in dynamics and $n_1 - n_2$ and $n_3 - n_4$ do not or if
c. (Articulation) the transition $n_2 - n_3$ involves a change in articulation and $n_1 - n_2$ and $n_3 - n_4$ do not or if
d. (Length) n_2 and n_3 are of different lengths and both pairs n_1 and n_2, and n_3 and n_4 do not differ in length.

Proximity and change apply locally, but the boundaries extend higher in the hierarchy where the conditions are more intense. This can refer to a boundary supported by both proximity and change or to a boundary at which one of those conditions is more pronounced than the adjacent segmentations.

GPR 4 (Intensification) Where the effects picked out by GPRs 2 and 3 are relatively more pronounced, a larger-level group boundary may be placed.

Symmetry is one of the most important analytical conditions in tonal music, but music without an even meter mostly leans away from symmetrical forms and constructions. However, most music includes some sort of similarities, considered within these rules as parallelism. Groups might contain a parallel contour or begin in parallel ways, but they often cannot be meaningfully divided into segments of equal length. As such, I have reordered the following two rules and suggested that symmetry operates weakly. Parallelism is a more salient feature without a perceptible meter. I omit the final rule in GTTM, GPR 7, which addresses the aspects of the theory outside the scope of this work.

GPR 5 (Parallelism) Where two or more segments of the music can be construed as parallel, they preferably form parallel parts of groups.

GPR 6 (Symmetry) Weakly prefer grouping analyses that most closely approach the ideal subdivision of groups into two parts of equal length.

These GWFRs and GPRs guide the first step of my analyses. Each group contains perceptually salient events that contribute to a hierarchy. Whereas temporal structure in tonal music depends heavily on meter to describe the points of perceptual emphasis, I depict a prominence structure informed by stress theory in lieu of applying GTTM's metrical structure.

3.4 Prominence Structure

Metrical structure outlines the pattern of strong and weak beats inferred by listeners that forms the temporal scaffold to which they relate musical sounds (Lerdahl & Jackendoff 1983: 12). This structure comprises beats evenly spaced in time; as well, the notated meter ideally remains constant throughout the piece. GTTM states that beats must be equally spaced in time and that meter must be periodic, and music without these qualities cannot be heard as being metered. Metrical structure is also hierarchical. The smallest level of metrical structure corresponds to the smallest rhythmic subdivision at that point of the piece.

GTTM's MWFRs state that every attack point must be associated with a beat at the smallest metrical level, beats must be present at all smaller hierarchical levels, strong beats at each level must be placed two or three beats apart, and the tactus and immediately larger levels must consist of evenly spaced beats. The tactus is the level of metrical structure on which most people focus, for instance, the level at which "the conductor waves his baton, the listener taps his foot, and the dancer completes a shift in weight" (Lerdahl & Jackendoff 1983: 21). The listener's sensitivity to metrical perception is strongest at the tactus level and weaker when attending to subdivisions and larger divisions. As such, composers can include irregular structures at very high and very low levels without disrupting the listener's sense of meter; meter is a relatively local phenomenon (Lerdahl & Jackendoff 1983: 21). MPRs state a preference for parallel structures, beats that align with the inception of pitch events, beats that align with relatively long notes or patterns of articulations, and structures in which strong beats appear relatively early. Other rules account for cadences, suspensions, and bass lines. As shown in Ex. 14, metrical structure can meaningfully describe

structure in tonal music, such as the Beethoven excerpt shown previously. Beats
are indicated by dots below the staff that line up with the notated music. The
lowest level of the structure is spatially the top line, closest to the staff, and
larger levels progress outward. Here, the smallest level of metrical structure is
the eighth note, present in m. 3.

The largest level contains a beat every four measures, beginning in the second
measure to align upcoming cadences with higher levels. Higher levels are
theoretically present, but listeners are unlikely to perceive them because of
the long duration between such large beats. This excerpt shows the typical
saliency of the first beat in each measure, with the third beat being the next-most
prominent. The structure displays evenness throughout, and the largest metrical
level in the example repeats every four measures.

Metrical structure as described does not pertain to all post-tonal music.
Although meter is a relatively local phenomenon, I am interested in analyzing
music that often lacks an even tactus. For instance, such music displays constantly changing notated meters, which makes metrical perception unlikely. To
illustrate the difficulty of describing post-tonal music through metrical structure, I have reproduced an excerpt from Hyla's *DOI3* in Ex. 15. Although the
meters 3/4 and 4/4 in the first two measures can be divided into quarter notes,
2/4 and the additive time signature of 3/4+1/16 cannot be divided into evenly
spaced beats larger than a sixteenth note, which is much too fast to be

Example 14 Beethoven Cello Sonata No. 3, mm. 1–6: metrical and grouping
structure

Example 15 *DOI3* mm. 155–163, cello: application of metrical structure

considered a tactus. The dots represent as faithful an application of metrical structure as possible, which ultimately does not elucidate anything helpful.

This analysis displays the sixteenth-note level throughout the excerpt for ease of comparison. The first two measures are parallel in structure but have different time signatures, immediately presenting a problem because the half-note level contains beats spaced both two and three beats apart. The half-note level either aligns with the downbeat of m. 157 according to the notated meter or with the third beat of m. 156 according to parallelism, which would lead to an unlikely emphasis of the quarter-note triplets at the beginning of the next measure. Measure 157 mixes quarter-note triplets with dotted eighth- and sixteenth-note durations, which do not share a metrical beat below a half note. Measures 159–160 mix triple, quadruple, and quintuple subdivisions, and the 2/8+1/8 meter (m. 160) excludes the possibility of evenness above the eighth-note level.

Another primary issue is that MPR 3 states a preference for beats to align with the inception of pitch events, but dotted and tied rhythms displace the inceptions of notes from the notated beats; the second and last notes of m. 162 exemplify this. The first note of m. 160 shows this conflict because MPR 5 aligns strong beats with notes of relatively long duration. The low C in m. 160 should be a strong beat because it is long in relation to the surrounding notes, yet the inception of the note is displaced from the notated downbeat by a triplet eighth note. I chose to include mm. 155–158 here to show how metrical structure does not describe the measures even though they are divisible by a quarter note.

Metrical structure outlines points of perceptual salience that do not apply to a description of post-tonal music; the analysis in Ex. 15 is ineffective due to several insurmountable issues and conflicts. Motivations behind the MPRs do apply, but the rules themselves do not. Meter as a perceptual phenomenon requires evenness or periodicity in the tactus level, but the notated meter in music without a periodic beat is alternatively a tool for segmenting the musical surface that is not perceived by the audience; without a tactus to establish periodicity, "no sense of meter is possible" (London 2012: 15). Every written downbeat is not necessarily perceptually prominent, so the music does not engender a sense of recurring meter. Perceived meter gives the listener a pattern against which to relate rhythms, and the musical surface is either aligned or offset with the perceptual construct. Non-isochronous temporal structures require listeners to conceptualize rhythms in relation to a different perceptual structure.

I do not assume that listeners impose regularity on hearing metrically uneven music. I recognize prominence as the factor operating in lieu of a perceived meter and gesture as defining the relationship of the surface to the underlying structure. For instance, syncopation is defined as a stressed event occurring on a weak beat, with the beat hierarchy determined by the metrical structure. No performance features perfectly even temporal execution, but listeners still hear meter within the slight variations. Beyond slight deviations in live performance, listeners can infer temporal regularity from an irregular signal. Spoken English is an example of a rhythmically variable signal from which listeners extrapolate rhythmic structure through the perception of linguistic stress. The concept helps delineate the underlying temporal structure without even meter.

3.4.1 Metrical Stress Theory

In order to outline the underlying structure, stress theory provides an approach from linguistics. Emphasis in language manifests as stress, and the issue of emphasis in music without an even or periodic meter can be approached through a linguistic theory to replace the MWFRs and MPRs. I call this aspect of my work *prominence structure*, which describes perceptual prominence of musical events based on analogous operations within spoken language. The primary perceptual markers of linguistic stress are pitch contour, duration, and loudness, none of which are peculiar to language, so stress can translate to music.

The central claim of stress theory is that stress is the manifestation of rhythmic structure in language such that "every utterance has a rhythmic structure which serves as an *organizing framework* for that utterance's phonological and phonetic realization," so the underlying structure is similar to the effect of meter in music even though the rhythm is not necessarily even (Hayes 1995: 8). Stress is hierarchical, similar to GTTM's grouping and metrical structure. Theoretically, there is no limit to the number of levels of stress in English, but the differences between adjacent levels become less distinguishable with more levels of stress. Stress is assigned to each syllable, not to any smaller unit of language such as the phoneme, mora, vowel, or consonant. In English, stress is lexically designated, meaning there are not broad rules that designate stress on a certain syllable in a word, such as stress on the penultimate syllable of most words in Polish (Hayes 1995: 31). Stress depends on a larger context than only the immediately preceding and following syllables.

Linguistic stress theory begins with the metrical foot as the smallest unit at the smallest level. Feet are typically composed of two syllables or morae with either left or right emphasis. The bracketed grid notation involves a grouping structure and a rhythmic hierarchy of beats written above the text. The notation denotes stressed syllables with an /x/ at each level, and stressless syllables at the lowest layer are marked with a /./. Groups, referred to as domains, are enclosed by parentheses. Thus, metrical feet appear as either (x .) for a left-headed foot or

(. x) for a right-headed foot. In this notation, a foot encompasses two levels that combined into one, a first level marking each event with dots and a second level to show stress with each /x/.

Feet are grouped into domains at the phrase level, and the head of the domain is assigned stress in the next level. Domains at the next level are then formed, and the heads of those domains are stressed, and so on. This process is analogous to WFRs in GTTM in that it yields many different possible results. As such, the results must be constrained to preferable outcomes. Stress theory lists several rules that are essential to the codification of my method below.

Example 16 shows an analysis of the sentence, "Belgian farmers grow turnips." In this example, each foot corresponds to a word. The stressed syllables in each foot are designated lexically, and higher levels are determined according to sentence structure, as shown in Ex. 17 in which each level of the stress analysis is colored the same as the corresponding layer of the sentence diagram. This sentence could be spoken with different stress patterns in order to highlight "nonnormative focus on a particular word" such as emphasizing the first word to indicate which specific farmers grow turnips (Lerdahl 2001: 339). However, the following realization generated from the grammatical structure generally holds true.

Stress theory begins with feet as the smallest units, but I do not rely on the foot as an organizational unit. Rather, my framework is constructed from the

```
(                    x       )
(        x     )(        x       )
( x   . )( x    . )(  x  )( x   . )
```
Belgian farmers grow turnips

Example 16 Application of metrical stress theory[13]

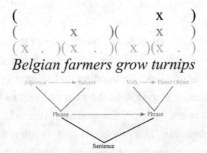

Belgian farmers grow turnips

Example 17 Stress analysis with correspondingly colored sentence diagram

---

[13] Example reproduced from Hayes 1995: 369.

unit of the gesture. Whereas listeners can hear and feel a regular pulse, the heard structure in music without a perceptible meter relies on gesture when the music lacks evenness. The aesthetic of gestures relies on several musical aspects, incorporating the analytically undervalued "pacing, dynamics, and articulation," with qualities such as "rhythm and meter, melody and motive, harmony and tonality, phrase structure and form" (Hatten 2010: 50). Analysis of gestures requires the integration of factors "outside the parameters of rhythm, meter, or pitch," which I consider as the perception of stress and emphasis (Chittum 1971: 23). Analysis of prominence to illuminate the underlying temporal structure requires the synthesis and balance of several musical factors to outline the heard structure.

3.4.2 Prominence Structure Rules

Prominence structure is the hierarchy of perceptual salience of events, employing the combination of grouping structure with fills the role of metrical structure, so the prominence well-formedness rules (PWFRs) are reflective of the MWFRs. The notation begins with grouping denoted by brackets and prominence denoted with the letter /x/, and the unstressed events at the lowest level are indicated with a /./. Mirroring MWFR 1, which states that every attack point must be associated with a beat at the smallest metrical level, my first rule articulates that every attack point must be assigned prominence at the lowest level. Because I am focusing on the phrase level, specific phrases might have different numbers of hierarchical levels, depending on the context. Hayes notes that five levels of stress seem to be the maximum listeners can perceive. Others have hypothesized as few as three and as many as five (Hayes 1995: 21–22). I aim for three to four levels of prominence with the understanding that a different number of levels might be appropriate in different contexts.

PWFR 1 Every attack point must be associated with a point in the smallest level of the prominence hierarchy present at that point in the piece.

In linguistics, *culminativity*[14] is the quality that every word or phrase contains one strongest syllable, which contains the primary stress. In English, stress is culminative at the word, phrase, and possibly higher levels. At the word level, this applies to phonological rather than grammatical words. For example, "the" is often grouped with the following content word, so "the farmer" would function as a single phonological word that comprises two grammatical words; "farm-" would be the syllable bearing the greatest stress. Within the development of my rules, the concept of culminativity directs that every group

---

[14] Throughout this discussion, I have italicized the concepts from metrical stress theory.

has a single note that is assigned the greatest prominence at each level. Further, this applies to the concept of gesture in that certain notes are analogously grouped with their neighbors, especially very fast notes, which is why gestures can contain more than three notes in a row that are not perceived as prominent.

PWFR 2 Each group contains a single note bearing the greatest prominence at every level present at that point in the piece.

Hatten states that gestures are hierarchical in nature, and PWFR 3 supports the logistics of such a construction. The *continuous column constraint* states that a unit stressed at one level is also stressed at all lower levels, which protects from prominence skipping a layer. As well, the *law of downward implication* states that beats at high levels in the structure must also be beats at all lower levels. These concepts match MWFR 2 and are reflected in PWFR 3.

PWFR 3 Every point of prominence at a given level must also be a point of prominence at all smaller levels present at that point in the piece.

To protect from stress clashes or consecutive syllables bearing the same level of emphasis, *lack of assimilation* describes that a stressed syllable does not generate prominence on immediately adjacent syllables. This typically results in patterns of alternating degrees of stress, which is reminiscent of the assertion of MWFR 3 that strong beats must be spaced two or three beats apart at each level. This sense of alternation between strong and weak events is addressed in PWFR 4. Because gestures do not invariably contain the same number of events, strongly and weakly prominent events can alternate without being evenly spaced in time.

PWFR 4 Any two adjacent points of prominence must not both be points of prominence at the immediately larger level.

Whereas a language's grammar dictates the specific placement and interactions of stress, I address prominence through the interaction of musical features. The three attributes of sound in order of perceptual prominence are pitch contour, duration (referred to as "length" in GTTM), and loudness. These three variables form the basis of the first three PRs. The rest of the rules are derived from stress theory with consideration of the motivations behind the MPRs.

As the strongest factor in perception of emphasis, pitch contour offers a basis for the first PR. This applies within gestures, but the concept is also salient at larger levels. Because stress in language is not invariably correlated to pitch height, this rule allows for either high or low pitches to be recognized as prominent. The following examples are excerpted from the cello part of Hyla's *DOI3*. In Ex. 18, the C# and the E are the highest notes in their respective gestures and are consequently both marked as heads. The E is prominent at a higher level in part because it is higher in pitch than the C#.

PPR 1 (Pitch Contour) Prefer a prominence structure in which a pitch at the high or low extreme of the pitch contour within a group is prominent.

Example 18 *DOI3* m. 165, cello: lowest two levels of prominence structure
Notes with proportionally long durations are heard as prominent, so the attack points associated with them are preferably associated with greater prominence. In Ex. 18 above, the analysis of the C# and E is reinforced by the fact that they have the longest durations within their respective gestures, and the E is relatively longer than the C#. The second group in this example also shows how several relatively fast notes represent a gesture rather than attempting to create feet by parsing the music into pairs of notes. Such an analysis would be perceptually irrelevant, but the concept of stressed and unstressed events informs my methodology.

PPR 2 (Duration) Prefer a prominence structure in which greater prominence aligns with attack points of events with proportionally longer duration than the surrounding events.

Although volume is not as salient of a factor as the previous two, it signals a small degree of stress in language; louder events are weakly associated with greater prominence. Example 19 shows an instance in which Hyla specifically indicates prominence through loud dynamics. Emphasis can also align with a softer volume upon a sudden change of dynamic or an interruption of a crescendo, but this is defined in another rule that addresses change (PPR 5).

The second measure begins with a grace note marked *fortissimo*, which distinguishes it as the head of the gesture, even though a prominent grace note is an unexpected construction. This occurs directly after a *pianissimo* gesture, which is considered within the same group at the middle level. Because of the

Example 19 *DOI3* mm. 5–6, cello: volume indicating prominence

louder dynamic, the grace note is assigned prominence at the second level. Loudness functions locally within gestures and on a larger scale between heads of gestures. However, the fact that the second gesture is louder than the first does not necessarily mean the gesture is entirely more prominent, just that the head is more prominent. This example also illustrates how notated meter is not necessarily a salient factor in the structure; the grace note is perceptibly more prominent than the downbeat it precedes.

PPR 3 (Loudness) Weakly prefer a prominence structure in which loud volume is associated with greater prominence.

According to GTTM, stress is related to accent, and PPR 4 is derived from this viewpoint. Accented notes draw greater attention from the listener, particularly without an even meter around which to create a sense of syncopation. As such, prominence preferably aligns with notes marked with an accent. Example 20 exemplifies the connection between prominence and accent.

PPR 4 (Accent) Prefer a prominence structure in which accented events are prominent in proportion with the strength of the accents.

An accent draws attention because it gives the attack point a different quality than the surrounding events. Similarly, a sudden change in any musical characteristic is perceptually salient. MPR 5 references this, with a preference for metrically strong beats at the inception of different articulations, but this also applies to sudden changes in rhythmic durations, dynamics, texture, and timbre. This rule particularly supports other rules, as shown in Ex. 21. The downbeat C in the second measure is accented and is the highest pitch within its gesture, but it is also the inception of a pattern of rhythm (dotted-sixteenth, dotted-sixteenth, sixteenth) and articulation lasting three quarter notes. The change to this pattern, accent, and high pitch make the C prominent in the second and third levels as well. This example is an excerpt of a larger structure, so the left edge of the top level is not visible here.

PPR 5 (Change) Prefer a prominence structure in which a relatively prominent beat occurs at the inception of a new

a. pattern of articulation,
b. pattern of rhythmic durations,

Example 20 *DOI3* m. 161, cello: accent giving prominence in a gesture

Example 21 *DOI3* mm. 165–166, cello: prominence associated with change

Example 22 *DOI3* mm. 159–160, cello: parallelism in prominence structure

c. dynamic,
d. texture, and
e. timbre.

PPR 6 draws attention to the importance of parallelism, suggesting that parallelism is perceptually salient. The rule is a reflection of MPR 1. The lowest level of the prominence structure in Ex. 22 shows that the low C is the head of both gestures. The rhythms and notes are not the same in both measures, but the upward contour, initial low C's, and the recurrence of this gesture in subsequent measures support that they should be interpreted with parallel structures.

PPR 6 (Parallelism) Where two or more groups or parts of groups can be construed as parallel, they preferably receive parallel prominence structure.

In establishing a hierarchy of emphasis, the *end rule* suggests that stress aligns with either the left- or rightmost element. However, stress is moved inward from the end if the element at the edge does not branch, meaning that the rightmost stressed syllable is not followed by another syllable or the leftmost syllable is not preceded by another syllable. The end rule applies even if there are syllables following or preceding the rightmost or leftmost syllables if they are considered *extrametrical* or outside the rhythmic pattern. This influences my analyses because prominence can shift inward if the attack points following or preceding the event in question are only associated with dots at the lowest level of the prominence structure.

PPR 7 (End Rule) Weakly prefer a prominence structure in which prominence aligns with the leftmost or rightmost event of a group. Prefer that prominence is moved

a. one event to the right if the prominent event is on the left edge and is not preceded by any attack points with prominence greater than the lowest level or

b. one event to the left if the prominent event is on the right edge and is not followed by any attack points with prominence greater than the lowest level.

Linguistic stress tends toward *rhythmic distribution* such that syllables with the same level of stress tend to be spaced roughly equally. However, this distribution is never perfectly even, as indicated by the previously shown "cats chase birds" example. This is an approximate tendency rather than a requirement. Hearing speech, listeners tend to perceive even stresses within an uneven signal, imposing a regular rhythm on the sound (Hayes 1995: 31). GTTM also notes that meter is not performed perfectly evenly but that slight variations do not disturb the listener's sense of meter. From the perspective of GTTM, metrical structure within language would be considered non-isochronous and aperiodic with a tendency toward evenness.[15] PPR 8 addresses this tendency toward evenness, as shown in Ex. 23 applied at the gesture level. Because even rhythmic distribution is not a common feature in music with uneven meter, this rule is weakly applicable.

PPR 8 (Distribution) Weakly prefer a prominence structure in which prominent events on the same level are roughly equally spaced apart in time.

Both downbeats, D and C, are prominent because they are at their respective extremes of the pitch contour and follow parallelism with other local gestures. The head of the second gesture in m. 162 could be interpreted as the first C in the group, supported by the accent and articulation pattern, but the Bb is more prominent because of the relative duration to the C and because it aligns with rhythmic distribution of emphasis. Prominence on the Bb results in equidistance between the three heads marked in the example, which are reminiscent of an ephemeral tactus.

Example 23 presents a situation in which prominence on the F# is feasible because it is relatively long and at the edge of the pitch contour. However, it clashes with the adjacent low C, which is unquestionably prominent. The heard structure is affected by such conflicts. In language, stress clashes are instances at the phrase and sentence levels of adjacent events with equal levels of stress.

Example 23 *DOI3* mm. 162–163, cello: tendency toward rhythmic distribution

---

[15] The word "meter" is defined differently within the domains of music and linguistics, but I use the term exclusively in the musical sense.

Example 24 *DOI3* mm. 162–163, cello: musical analog of rhythm rule

Stress theory posits several processes by which clashes are resolved, and these guide the following discussion of how to address situations that yield adjacent events with equal levels of prominence.

The primary tool by which stress clashes are solved is called *move x*, with the /x/ referring to the grid marks denoting stress. Only one /x/ can move along its level at a time, preventing two grid marks on different levels from moving together to resolve a clash. Movement must occur on the level at which the clash occurs. A related mechanism is the *rhythm rule*, which suggests that stress shifts leftward when a stronger stress is present. This is more ubiquitous in language than in music, but the concept is reflected in the distribution process of PPR 8. For example, the word "thirteen" has lexically designated stress assigned to the second syllable (thirtéen) when spoken alone. In the phrase "thirteen men," the two adjacent stresses on "-teen" and "men" would clash, so the stress on "-teen" moves leftward to "thír-." The phrase would be pronounced as "thírteen mén."

Example 24 presents a musical analysis reflecting this concept at the second level of the hierarchy.

Whereas the B appears to be stressed at the second level because of the accent and the downward pitch contour landing on the note, prominence on the B would clash with the following C downbeat. This shifts the initial prominence structure of 1 ... 2 ... 3 to 2 ... 1 ... 3. The prominence on the C cannot shift because only one /x/ can move at a time, and the C is prominent at the third level; shifting the /x/ on only the second level would create an ill-formed structure. As such, the /x/ above the B shifts leftward to the D.

Finally, *destressing* is the process by which the weaker of two stresses is removed in the context of a stress clash. Rather than elevating the strong stress, the weaker stress is reduced, and this process also applies to prominence structure. Having established the rules guiding my analytical approach, I will present example analyses in the next section.

4 Analyses

I present analyses excerpted from four pieces. Because *DOI3* inspired the exploration that led to my analytical framework, this section begins by analyzing three excerpts of the piece to show the practical application of my theory. I dissect the three excerpts to show how to apply my analytical system and solve issues encountered, developing the system as well as addressing the structure of the excerpts. Following these *DOI3* excerpts, I provide example analyses of three excerpts from three other composers.

4.1 Lee Hyla – *Dream of Innocent III*

4.1.1 Excerpt 1: mm. 159–166

DOI3 is scored for amplified cello, piano, and percussion, and the augmented cello sound equalizes the volume of the three instruments (Hyla 1987). The piece is structured in three large sections, with cello solos functioning as transitions in between. Although all three instruments participate in the drama, the cello is the protagonist of the work.

The first excerpt, mm. 159–166, includes most of the examples used to illustrate the PPRs. This section contains non-isochronous meter and is centered around the open C string as a foundation for upward arpeggiations interspersed with short melodic material akin to "licks." Temporal features that elude evenness include changes in the time signature between every measure, a tempo range of quarter note = 88–92, and a notated rhythmic disruption of a comma in parentheses (m. 159). Although this section includes sparse piano and percussion, I have chosen to show only the cello part because it is the most musically salient line at this point in the piece. Later excerpts come from the two cello solos.

My analysis begins with grouping structure shown in Ex. 25. Groups at the lowest level are almost all determined according to the proximity of notes as stated in GPR 2. However, m. 162 segments into two groups that begin in parallel ways with two repeated notes followed by a descending major third supported by GPR 5, and there is a change in articulation to support the boundary according to GPR 3. The entire measure could be viewed as a single group at the lowest level, but I do not believe there would be a single prominent note within such a contoured line of notes with variable durations. The measure undoubtedly forms a group at the second level, but my grouping analysis reflects the immediate context; the group in m. 161 at the lowest level is not as substantial as the entirety of m. 162, so the grouping boundary in the middle of m. 162 matches with the straightforward contours of the surrounding groups at the lowest level.

Measure 165 is also divided into two groups by a boundary supported by a change in register and articulation (GPR 3), distance between attack points (GPR 2), and parallelism of downward contour (GPR 5). The segmentations in m. 166 at the end of the excerpt yield several groups based on parallelism. The first three groups in the measure comprise identical rhythms and contour, signaled as an important gestural feature in the previous measure. Parallelism is strongly supported in the heard structure (GPR 5). The final group in the measure varies in rhythm but contains the same contour, representing a rhythmic augmentation of the first two notes of the previous gestures that still signals parallelism.

Larger-level boundaries are also suggested by parallelism. At the middle level, the groups in mm. 159 and 163 are closely related and initiate the beginning of groups at the second level according to parallelism; mm. 161 and 164 are similar except for an added rest (m. 164), and they are in parallel locations at the ends of groups at the second level. With these groups segmented, the intervening material (m. 162) forms a separate group flanked by rests that result in long durations between attack points. The repeating rhythms of the groups in m. 166 warrant their cohesion as a second-level group, giving the listener a brief experience of a pulse that is interrupted at the end of the measure. The final two eighth notes are maintained as a group at the second level because the interruption of the ephemeral pulse is a perceptually salient event. At the highest level, all three groups begin with the note C and end with a downward contour.

The resulting construction of each measure as a group at the first or second level of the hierarchy supports that Hyla tailored the notation to match the organization of the musical surface. Groups are not structured with symmetrical

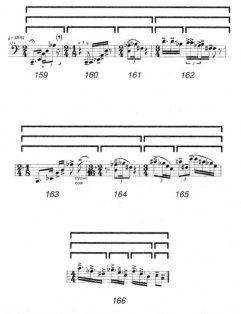

Example 25 *DOI3* mm. 159–166, cello: grouping structure

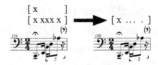

Example 26 *DOI3* m. 159, cello: prominence structure notation
simplification

lengths, and parallelism functions rhythmically and with pitch content as contour and specific pitch classes. The separation of groups by rests resembles spoken phrases.

I imply four levels of perceptual prominence. Although the notation displays three levels of brackets, the lowest notated layer represents two levels of prominence to avoid redundancy in the grouping structure. Example 26 shows the consolidation of the notation.

On the left, each event is marked at the lowest level, and the second level contains the head of the group. As the left side shows, the grouping structure remains the same at the first and second levels of prominence. The notation can be simplified to combine the lowest two prominence levels in order to avoid a redundant grouping structure and to draw greater visual focus to the prominent events.

Parallelism functions in the prominence structure of mm. 159–166, reproduced in Ex. 27,[16] but several of the other PPRs exert significant influence. Many of the issues at the bottom level have been addressed in the discussion of the rules themselves. At the second notated level, the low C in m. 159 is prominent due to its pitch at the bottom of the contour (PPR 1) and its relatively long length caused by the fermata (PPR 2). The low C in m. 163 is also prominent at the second level, reinforced by parallelism to match the beginning of the excerpt (PPR 6). Avoiding a stress clash with this downbeat suggests emphasis on the D in m. 162. In the formally parallel group, a possible stress clash results in the C# downbeat (m. 165) as prominent at the second level. This layout is supported by the marked accent on the C#. The downbeat of the final measure is the head of its group because it has the highest pitch (PPR 1) and marks the beginning of a drastic change in articulation and rhythmic pattern (PPR 5). The head of the group at the very end (m. 166) also extends to the second level to maintain a well-formed structure. At the top level, a parallel construction is reflected in the heads being the first note of each group, all of which are the pitch class C.

---

[16] EX. 27 does not contain any dynamics in the score, so dynamics are not a part of the prominence structure.

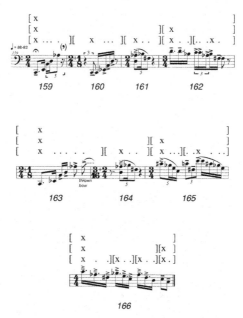

Example 27 *DOI3* mm. 159–166, cello: prominence structure

This analysis shows a pattern in the temporal structure without evenness. Each of the three groups begins with its most prominent note. Columns with the same number of /x/'s are not adjacent above the lowest line. The sense of alternation within the multiple levels of the hierarchy mirrors that of GTTM's metrical structure but without evenness in the rhythms that would project a meter. Complete prominence structures, such as Ex. 27, can be difficult to read, so I have included accompanying gradient barcodes that visually represent the prominence structure. In Ex. 28, each gradient section represents a group at the lowest level, with the amount of space between sections corresponding to how high the boundary extends; the note at the darkest part of the gradient corresponds to the most prominent within the group, with darker colors representing prominence extending to higher levels. These diagrams are simply a visual representation intended to help the reader see the structure more immediately and function as visual maps of phrasing for performers, showing the energetic shaping of each gesture.

For the purposes of comparing prominence structures, tree diagrams provide a more useful visual tool. The following discussion describes how my analyses translate into tree diagrams. Each analysis will thus include three representations of structure: prominence structure with /x/'s and /./'s, a visual translation as a gradient barcode, and a tree diagram to compare structures to each other. Used in several fields, such as mathematics, tree diagrams show visual

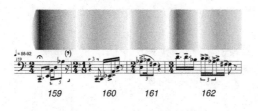

159   160   161   162

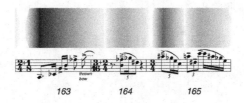

163   164   165

166

Example 28 *DOI3* mm. 159–166, cello: gradient barcode showing
prominence structure

representations of strength and weakness within hierarchical relationships.
GTTM uses tree diagrams to show prolongational reductions, but I present
trees to represent different information. I translate prominence structure into
tree notation for ease of visualizing the similarities and patterns in the structure.
The creation of the diagrams is best viewed from the bottom to top. Where two
lines meet at a node, the line from the stronger event continues upward, and the
line from the weaker event terminates. Example 29 shows how prominence
structure translates into a tree diagram.

The note with three /x/'s in the structure links with line *A*, which extends to
the very top (line *A*). This event receives the greatest level of prominence
because its line extends the highest. Line *B* is the next-most prominent note
because it is the second-tallest line; it represents the note with two /x/'s. Each
line *C* connects to the head of the groups at the smallest level and corresponds to
notes marked with a single /x/. Only notes that represent the head of their groups
are connected to lines; the notes marked with /./'s are not connected with lines.
This representation allows for a quick comparison of structure as the number
and direction of branches are immediately apparent. The cornerstones of the
structure, or the most prominent notes, are easily identified within the larger

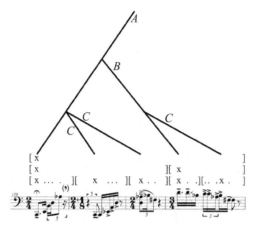

Example 29 Prominence structure translated to tree diagram

context by the tallest lines. My use of trees and brackets is analogous to that of Chomsky's in *Syntactic Structures*, in that the branching corresponds to the bracketing because tree branches connect with the head of each bracket. However, there is a plethora of ways to represent this information in various types of branching and tree diagrams.

Example 30 contains the prominence structure of mm. 159–166 of *DOI3* translated into a tree diagram. The three tallest lines extend from the top to the three prominent C's, followed by right-branching to the notes marked with two /x/'s. The first two trees are identical except for the double branch in the first tree at the lowest level. However, this double branch is present in the third tree, similar to the other two except that the far-right line does not branch. The three structures contain only slight differences. The shared resemblances of the trees suggest a pattern in the underlying temporal structure that persists regardless of the absolute length of each segment of music. The final tree encompasses only eight notated eighth notes, while the first tree consists of nineteen eighth notes, and the musical material is not the same. Temporal structure is not dependent on motivic development or melodic content, although it can be related. In this example, the first two trees contain closely related material in the first parts, but the music in the second half of each is vastly different.

This visualization aids in the performance of the music because it shows the most perceptually salient notes. The events that do not connect to a line belong to the gestural level and should not be given temporal weight. I am not suggesting that these notes are unimportant or that accents on these notes should be disregarded. Rather, my analysis shows that they are not significant building blocks in the heard structure of this excerpt. This tree structure provides a layout

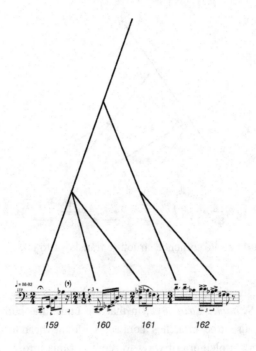

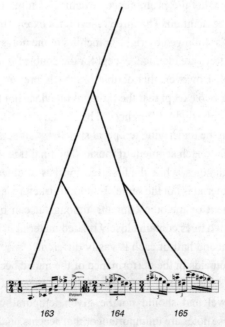

Example 30 *DOI3* mm. 159–166, cello: prominence structure as tree

166

Example 30 (cont.)

of perceptually important notes to suggest which events contextually form the basis of temporal structure.

4.1.2 Excerpt 2: mm. 74–89

Measures 74–89, reproduced in Ex. 31, represent the first half of the cello solo that occurs between the first two large sections of *DOI3*. This interjection is marked *con rubato*, so the excerpt lacks a fixed tempo. The dynamics remain soft, peaking at *mezzo forte*, which provides a contrast to the previous bombastic section involving the piano and percussion. The entire excerpt groups together and is followed by the stillest and softest note of the piece, to be held for ten seconds.

In this section, the protagonist of the piece, the cello, plays *subito mezzo forte* interjections, but the line is stymied by *subito piano* interruptions, eventually dissolving back into the initial motive with references to the beginning of the entire piece. The rhythmic augmentation enhances the feeling that the material is being held back. This aesthetic is also reflected in the pitch material; the second note matches pitch class and register of the final note, sealing the feeling that the intervening material is a winding exploration that goes nowhere.

Example 31 *DO13* mm. 74–89: grouping structure

The cello's calm struggle ends where it began, and the piano and percussion cannot help because the cello is playing alone for the first time in the piece.

Many of the grouping boundaries at the lowest level overlap as shown in Ex. 31, resulting from the disruptive quality of the quiet interjections. Loud licks with upward contours seem to be leading somewhere, but they are quickly redirected into the quieter world. For instance, mm. 79, 81, and 83 contain gestures leading into the following downbeats, which are actually the first notes of the subsequent groups. Changes in dynamics delineate boundaries in places such as the *subito mezzo forte* in mm. 79 and 83. The *crescendo* in m. 81 can function to connect softer and louder aesthetics, but even that fails. Boundaries at the second level exist at the points of more pronounced changes in dynamics and rhythmic patterns. Although mm. 85–86 are separated by a quarter note rest, the boundary does not extend to the second level because of the similarity between mm. 84–85 and 86–87; both pairs match in contour and share similar pitches. The proximity of the quasi-repetition suggests they belong to the same group at the second level, rather than straddle a boundary. Measure 88 is preceded by a rest with a fermata, which extends the boundary to the top level. The final group is maintained at the second level because the augmentation of the grace notes into eighth notes and the motive into long durations creates low-level groups that are too long to be related together as a single group at the second level.

As shown in Ex. 32, the motivic development of the first three notes is perceptually important to my analyses and to the narrative supported by the temporal structure. Each presentation undergoes rhythmic augmentation, beginning with a quarter note between the inceptions of the notes, then a half note, and finally a half note plus an eighth note.

Each of these statements also begins a group at the highest level of my analysis, so an understanding of their relationship to each other reinforces the parallelism of their positions at the beginning of large-level groups. Example 32a shows the first three notes, and Ex. 32b shows the same pitch relationships with the middle note transposed down an octave to reverse the contour and establish the shape for the third presentation. Example 32c shows the final statement containing ornamentation matching the beginning of the piece, which also undergoes rhythmic augmentation from grace notes to eighth notes.

GTTM states that the underlying structures of overlapped groups must be well-formed, and this applies to prominence structure as well. The following examples are excerpted from the prominence structure of this section (mm. 74–89) and build to its entire presentation. My discussion begins with the treatment of overlapped groups, four of which are present in this example. This can cause well-formedness issues, particularly if the event at the point of overlap is perceptually prominent. Every group must have one event as its head, so a prominent overlapped event must align with either the first or second group but not both. To indicate the group to which the prominence belongs, a parenthesis instead of a bracket indicates the end of a group that overlaps with another but has a different event as its head. For instance, the underlying structure of mm. 83–84 is shown in Ex. 33, coupled with its translation to my notation.

The downbeat of m. 84 is the head of the group that it begins because the previous group has a different head as indicated by parallelism with other previous gestures. An overlapped /x/ associates with the group enclosed by the bracket and does not function as the head of the group marked with a parenthesis. This distinction maintains well-formedness that also affects the tree structure. Lines branch differently according to which group is headed by the overlapped /x/.

This example shows one of the challenges of my framework. If I included more levels of analysis, I could show the salience of the final Eb on a level

Example 32 *DOI3* mm. 74–89: motivic development

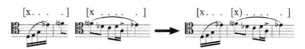

Example 33 *DOI3* mm. 83–84, cello: prominence in grouping overlap

Example 34 *DOI3* mm. 81–82, cello: prominence from change

Example 35 *DOI3* mm. 79–81, cello: prominence of F over longer Eb

between the two levels of /./ and /x/ shown here, allowing for a three tiered analysis. I chose to limit this example to two levels given the surrounding context of the larger phrase, but an isolated analysis of a shorter fragment could allow for the inclusion of more levels of prominence.

At the lowest level, one of the most salient factors affecting prominence is the sudden change in dynamics, register, and rhythmic values, as indicated by PPR 5. The previous example shows an interruption of louder and faster notes that begin in a starkly lower register, which also happens in mm. 79 and 81. Such immediate change suggests prominence on the first note of each gesture. The notes following the second two gestures are also prominent according to their relatively longer durations and their alignment with a suddenly softer dynamic, indicated as *subito piano*. The previous example shows this in operation, as does Ex. 34.

The other interruption, shown in m. 79 in Ex. 35, contains a parallel structure to the other two. Prominence in the second gesture of this example is pulled between the first F (high pitch, parallelism with the other two interruptions) and the Eb marked with a gray arrow (long duration). The rest of the *cantabile* gesture in Ex. 35 contains even eighth notes, so the Eb might stand out as contrasting, but the pitch is a neighbor between the initial and final F's of the gesture. In other gestures in this passage, there is a tension between F and Eb, so this is an example in which Hyla's approach to rhythm suggests harmonic tension. In all three interruptions, the F gains prominence, but Hyla's meticulous addition of a dot to the eighth note Eb references the final Eb, the longest note of the entire passage. The second level contains prominent F's in mm. 78, 80, 84, and 87 that are challenged by the note Eb, which is ultimately the most prominent in the final measure of the excerpt. This is another instance in which an extra level of analysis could show the prominence of the Eb, but I have limited this example to two levels given the complexity of analyzing a larger excerpt.

Duration is a salient factor throughout this passage. PPR 2 suggests prominence on the longest notes of the groups in mm. 75, 77, 88, and 89. However, Ex. 36 displays the priority of other factors in mm. 84–86. Parallelism with previous material suggests the downbeat F (m. 84) is prominent because it is at the top of the pitch contour with a *subito* dynamic, which overrides the longer duration of the quarter note Eb at the end of the group. The accented A also undermines the possibility of prominence on the Eb; the note is too short for the accent to override the prominence on the first F, but it is adjacent to the Eb and draws focus away from the longer duration. This represents one way in which Hyla suggests a harmonic tension between F and Eb in this excerpt. The second group in Ex. 36 displays a similar contour and rhythm to the previous group, so the first E is prominent instead of the final note in the group.

Articulation also undermines the prominence of Eb in Ex. 37 (mm. 78–79). In this example, the notes with the longest duration are F and Eb. Similar to Ex. 36, parallelism and pitch contour suggest prominence on the F, which is reinforced by the tenutos on C and Bb; dotted eighths with tenutos are close in duration to a quarter note, so the quarter note duration of the Eb does not sound significantly different. In contrast, the quarter note F sounds longer in its immediate context.

Prominence within the three statements of the primary motive shows how my framework elucidates the final presentation as the goal of the section. Example 38 shows the first two statements of the motive with the same prominence structure and three /x/'s on the first event, but the final statement has a different

Example 36 *DOI3* mm. 84–87, cello: prominence parallelism versus duration

Example 37 *DOI3* mm. 78–79, cello: articulation in prominence structure

underlying structure due to added notes and rhythmic augmentation that shifts prominence to the last note.

Prominence at the beginning of the third presentation only extends to the second level, as shown in Ex. 39, because of the long duration of the final Eb and because of the note's harmonic relevance. Ending on Eb supports the narrative of being stuck and resolves the underlying tension between F and Eb throughout the example. The final motivic statement is rhythmically augmented to the point that the final note and its ornamentation become a gesture of its own. Therefore, the first note of the motive, the F, is the head in the second level, but the Eb ultimately draws the focus at the highest level.

Within the complete excerpt (mm. 74–89, shown in Ex. 41), only three notes are marked with three /x/'s. The pitches match the initial three pitches of the motive, as shown in Ex. 40, although in a different order with the G#/Ab displaced by an octave. My analysis of perceptually prominent notes yields the same pitch collection as the primary motive of the section. Not only does this confirm the importance of the motive, but also it suggests that the performer treat the final statement differently by recognizing the Eb as a fundamental building block of the section as a whole.

Example 41 shows the entire prominence structure of the excerpt, from which the previous examples appear. Although Eb is a salient pitch, D and F are also

Example 38 *DOI3* mm. 74–89: motivic prominence

Example 39 *DOI3* mm. 88–89, cello: final motive prominence

Example 40 *DOI3* mm. 74–89: most prominent notes as motive

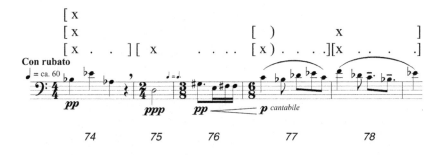

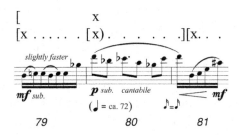

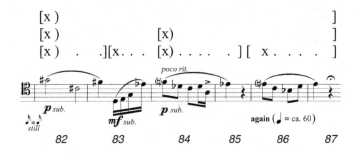

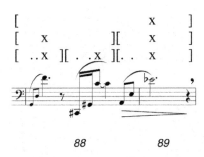

Example 41 *DO13* mm. 74–89, cello: prominence structure

perceived to be prominent throughout the excerpt. Previous examples outline the tension between Eb and F, but giving prominence to F and D suggests a harmonic approach of wavering around the Eb until the note is realized in the final measure. My methodology is not based on harmonic analysis, but I hope to show how the temporal structures could be used to delve into harmonic relationships within an excerpt. Hyla's conception of linear relationships to set up salient pitches could be a key to understanding his approach to harmony. The temporal structure suggests a tension between Eb and the two surrounding notes as a foundation of Hyla's approach to pitch in the excerpt.

The recurring upward sixteenth notes group with each following gesture because they all serve an anacrusis function. However, the distinctions are not always clear, and the decisions in my analyses reflect my own interpretation and application of the rules I have previously stated. Example 42 shows the prominence structure translated into a gradient barcode. Slanted divisions between gradient sections indicate grouping overlaps.

This excerpt displays three tree structures. Example 43 shows the first two trees, illustrating that the second tree is identical to the first upon removing the gray lines in the middle, even though the event durations and notated metric

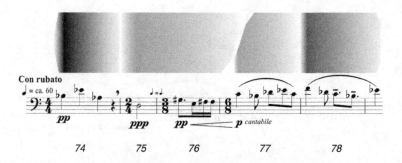

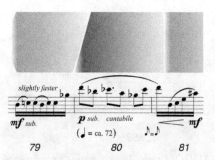

Example 42 *DOI3* mm. 74–89, cello: gradient barcode showing prominence structure

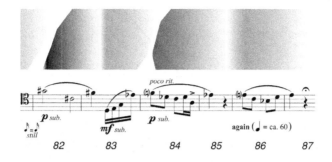

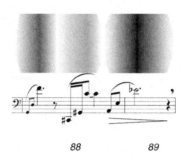

Example 42 (cont.)

divisions are different. The events encompassed within the gray branches are removed for the second tree, compressing the temporal layout of the overall structure. Each tree becomes successively less complex with fewer branches, supporting the narrative that the music is continually thwarted in its attempts to move ahead; it cannot develop, and sections are removed when it tries to develop.

The temporal structure in this excerpt shows Hyla's linear use of pitch to reinforce narrative and how his compositional approach involves the development and fragmentation of the underlying structure. Further testing would be required to see if these underlying structures might or might not be perceptible to the audience, but I believe the complexities of my analyses give the performers a perspective that aids in the performance of the music.

By analyzing Hyla's music in this way, listeners and performers can relate the temporal tension within his music in a broader context to see how the temporal flow affects the form and aesthetic of the music. The full prominence structure is shown in Ex. 44. The nuances within the first tree set up the rest of the excerpt as well as form the basis of structure in the second cello solo, the subject of the next analysis.

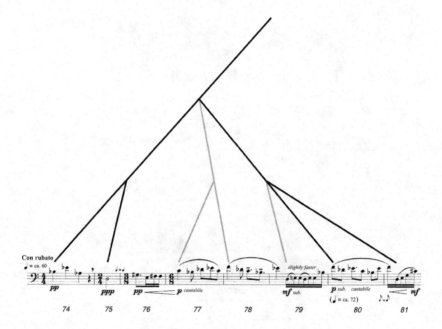

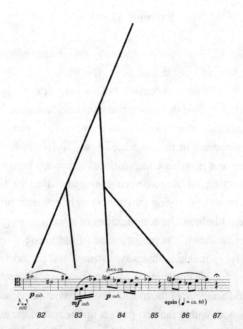

Example 43 *DOI3* mm. 74–89: prominence tree comparison

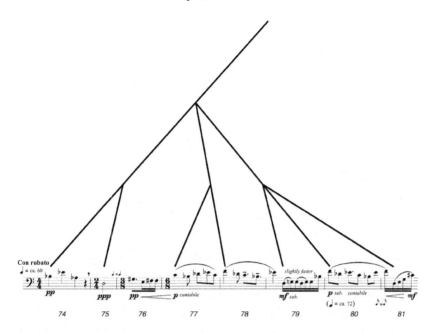

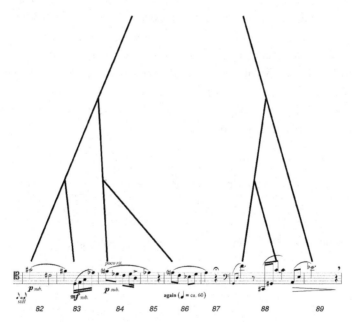

Example 44 *DOI3* mm. 74–89, cello: prominence structure as tree

4.1.3 Excerpt 3: mm. 203–205

Having analyzed the beginning of the first cello solo in *DOI3*, I now examine the corresponding part of the second cello solo, mm. 203–205. Aesthetically, the music is completely different. This is most immediately indicated by the dynamics; whereas *mezzo forte* was the loudest dynamic in the previous excerpt, the softest dynamic in this example is *fortissimo*. The increased energy indicated by the louder dynamics is also reflected in the greater number and speed of notes. While the first solo presented stymied material, this passage showcases the boisterousness of the cello as it refuses to back down. This excerpt is marked within three measures of free meter, so I have added reference letters to the following examples that correspond to the lowest level of grouping structure in order to facilitate my analysis.[17]

The lack of notated meter gives this excerpt an improvisatory feel. It requires that performers make crucial decisions about the grouping layout and temporal structure that can be addressed through the heard structure. The improvisatory aesthetic is enhanced by the grace notes and fast subdivisions throughout.

Generally, gestures at the lowest level of the grouping structure in this excerpt include many more notes than those found in the previous analyses. Parsing the groups shown in Ex. 45 into smaller entities would violate GPR 1 because the speed of performance renders smaller groups perceptually irrelevant, and Hyla's use of grace notes suggests they do not receive temporal weight in the structure. In the midst of fast notes, duration becomes a salient factor in establishing both grouping and prominence structures. For instance, longer durations mark the ends of groups *A*, *B*, *C*, *F*, *G*, and *L*, many of which are preceded by fast subdivisions or grace notes.

Example 45 *DOI3* mm. 203–205, cello: fast notes leading to long durations

---

[17] The published score shows one error, as confirmed by an examination of the manuscript: m. 205, beginning between *H* and *J*, is marked with the meter 4/8 in the published score, but there is no bar line after four eighth notes. The manuscript confirms this as a printing error, which I have corrected by omitting the time signature. The following five beamed notes are marked as sextuplet sixteenths, but the manuscript confirms this rhythmic demarcation is correct.

Example 46 *DOI3* mm. 203–205, cello: grouping and slight durational changes

Example 47 *DOI3* mm. 203–205, cello: grouping overlap, duration versus change

The structure of this excerpt establishes that grouping boundaries are delineated by longer notes, so even slight changes in duration initiate grouping boundaries such as those at the end of *E* and *H*, as shown in Ex. 46. The durations are not significantly longer than the surrounding notes, but even a slightly longer duration is perceptually salient in the midst of fast rhythms. The boundaries are further reinforced by register drops following both groups and a change in rhythmic subdivisions after *H* from sixteenth notes to sextuplets.

Change also supports the grouping boundaries at the ends of *B* (subito *fortissimo* taking the boundary into the second level) and *G* (register drop of two octaves). The end of *J* also extends to the second level due to a drop to the low C, initiating a climb back to the higher register. Each of these upward lines reinforces the raucous aesthetic of the passage. There are some instances where boundaries are not immediately obvious. In the overlap between *D* and *E*, the fermata on the C suggests a boundary before the A, but register change and parallelism suggest segmenting after the A. Example 47 shows that the groups overlap in order to account for the perceptually prominent factors of parallelism, duration, and register change.

The other grouping overlap in this excerpt occurs between *K* and *L*, isolated in Ex. 48. Both groups are within a single *crescendo*, and both contain an upward contour without a large register change in between. The rhythmic subdivision change from thirty-second notes to eighth notes on the Eb suggests a boundary after the Eb, but the tenuto and marked *molto vibrato sempre* indicates a change in tone color beginning with the Eb and therefore a boundary before the note. As such, the Eb is overlapped between the groups, but the

Example 48 *DOI3* mm. 203–205, cello: grouping overlap within changes

Example 49 *DOI3* mm. 203–205, cello: grouping structure

boundary does not extend to the second level because of the larger shape of the two gestures together.

The previous examples address grouping structure at the lowest level for all of the gestures within mm. 203–205, and Ex. 49 contains the grouping structure of the complete excerpt. Second level and third segmentations occur where changes are most pronounced and supported by duration.

Duration is also a salient factor in this prominence structure. Due to the abundance of fast notes in most of the gestures, longer notes emerge as perceptually prominent, and most of them are located at the end of each group. Except for group H, the longest notes are heads at the lowest level. In group *H* shown in Ex. 50, the initial *fortississimo* F is at the top of the pitch contour, which supercedes the slightly longer duration of the final note in the group. As well, emphasis on the F is more evenly distributed with the surround-ing points of prominence. As displayed in Ex. 50, group *D* is a parallel group,

Example 50 Nonparallel prominence of *H* and *D*

Example 51 Prominence within small durational variability

beginning with upward arpeggiated grace notes to the same F, but the groups do not have the same prominence structure. The F is a shorter note in group *D*, and the fermata suggests the final C as a point of prominence in the surrounding context. Starting with group *H*, the music drives forward to the final note of the excerpt. Because of this, prominence on the Eb at the end of *H* would be a disruption in the flow.

The continuation of fast rhythms immediately following *H* shows that the group does not need to display a parallel structure to *D*, which is subject to further issues. The final note of *D* is accented, but it is also shorter and softer than the preceding note C, so the C is heard as more prominent. Example 51 shows that group *J* also does not have much durational variability between the notes. The placement of the F at the peak of the pitch contour guides the prominence structure, reinforced by parallelism with other groups that end before a large registral drop.

Because the process for grouping overlaps might appear opaque, Ex. 52 shows the underlying structure of *K* and *L* and how my notation reflects it. In the example, both groups are presented as separate entities. When viewed separately, the final note of each group emerges as prominent. However, on the musical surface, the groups overlap on the shared E. In my notation, group *K* is enclosed by brackets (the bracket on the right side of the E), and group *L* begins with a parenthesis to show that the E is overlapped but is not the head of group *L*.

The only other event of group *K* that could sensibly be prominent is the first note of the group, but this would violate PWFR 4 because it would create an adjacent stress at the lowest level with the head of *J*. The low C would also be the only prominent one in the entire excerpt, so parallelism also supports the Eb as the head.

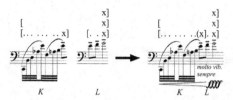

Example 52 Underlying prominence structure of *K* and *L*

Example 53 *DOI3* mm. 203–205, cello: prominence structure

Example 53 contains the complete prominence structure of mm. 203–205. Higher-level boundaries are strengthened by the dynamic notations. The first *fff* event of the passage, present in *B*, extends to the top level because it is also punctuated by a long duration. All of the events at the second level are within the same *fff* dynamic. The final note (G) of the excerpt is marked *ffff*, the loudest dynamic that Hyla uses in the entire piece. This is also the highest note of the excerpt, so it is prominent at the highest level because it is high, long, and loud. This passage continually pushes forward due to its constructions of groups that emphasize notes at the end and gestures with fast rhythms within unidirectional contours. Example 54 shows the gradient barcode.

The tree diagram in Ex. 55 confirms the tendency for final emphasis by showing several leftward branches in the structure. The tree also elucidates the tension between F and Eb present in the previous excerpt. With the

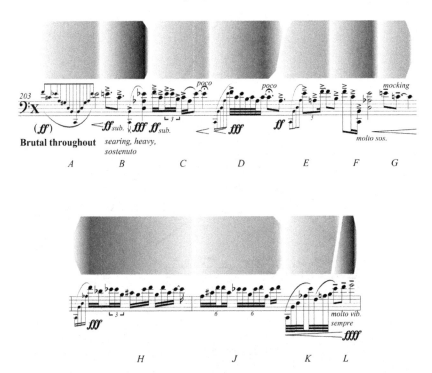

Example 54 *DOI3* mm. 203–205, cello: gradient barcode showing prominence structure

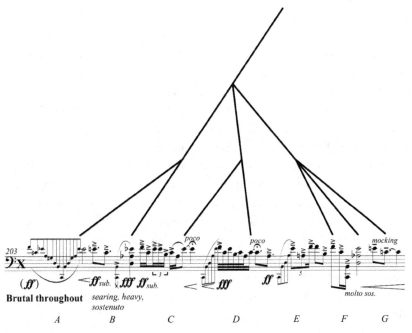

Example 55 *DOI3* mm. 203–205, cello: prominence structure as tree

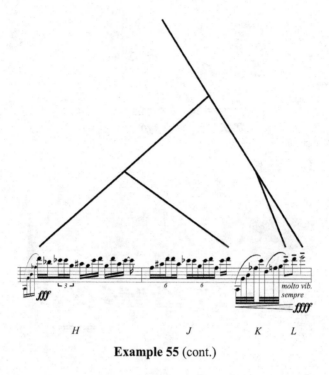

Example 55 (cont.)

exception of two C's in the first tree, all of the lines connect to F or Eb, pitches that ultimately resolve to G at the end of the excerpt.

By comparing this excerpt with Excerpt 2 from the first cello solo (Ex. 44), the larger implications of my analytical approach emerge. Example 56 reproduces Excerpts 2 and 3 (mm. 74–89 and 203–205, respectively), to show the relationship between the tree structures. The gray middle tree of Excerpt 2 is essentially a repetition of the first tree and is not present in Excerpt 3. The initial trees of both excerpts match except for the direction of the first branch at the lowest level. The final trees are also the same, except for an added branch at the lowest level in Excerpt 3, which I have colored gray.

Whether or not this underlying temporal relationship was consciously constructed, it serves as a grounding element of the composition. These excerpts exist in formally analogous positions as cello solos between the three larger ensemble sections. They have contrasting aesthetics and contain varying melodic and harmonic content, but the underlying structures are closely related. By hearing the related temporal structures in these excerpts, the listener perceives more coherence in the music. Further, this relationship exemplifies the function of gesture as the skeleton for expression in Hyla's music.

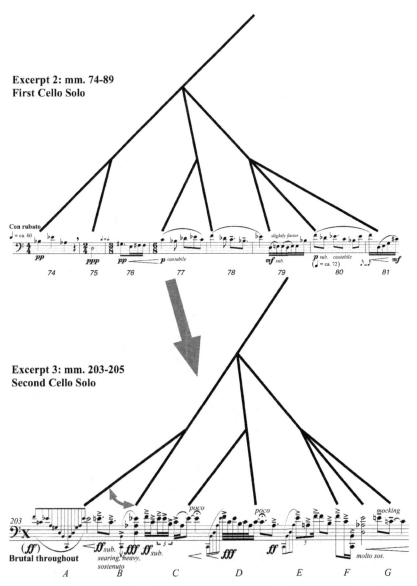

Example 56 Excerpts 2 and 3: prominence tree comparison

I have included three excerpts from *DOI3* to show how my system of analysis can be used to identify and compare underlying structures throughout a piece of music that contains sections without an even perceptible meter. My analyses show connections between materials that appear to be entirely distinct on the surface. As well, the three excerpts display commonly encountered issues with a detailed breakdown of solutions. I present the following three analyses by three

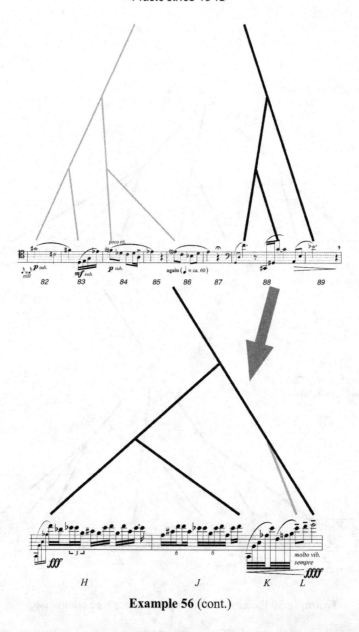

Example 56 (cont.)

composers other than Hyla, including two whose first languages are not English, to show more applications of the analytical system, rather than focusing on the construction of the system as with the Hyla examples. Although English is my first language, it is a tiny fraction of metrical stress theory, so my analytical system is not limited to music written by English-speaking composers; the principles of perception that form the foundation of my analyses are ubiquitous.

4.2 Tania León – *Four Pieces for Solo Cello, I*

Composer Tania León (b. 1943) is a pianist, composer, conductor, and educator dedicated to celebrating diversity and empowering all living composers.[18] Growing up in Havana, Cuba, León immigrated to the United States after earning a B.A. and an M.A. from Carlos Alfredo Peyrellade Conservatory, eventually landing in New York City. Her Cuban heritage has been an important artistic influence that first manifested in her *Four Pieces for Solo Cello* (1983), written after the death of her father. The piece uses several extended techniques throughout, and the third movement contains the most direct Cuban influence. Part of the contemporary aesthetic of the piece manifests in its complex temporal construction, including a wide array of varying subdivisions of the notated beat juxtaposed with sections of music that contain a very clear, even beat. My analysis focuses on the very opening of the unnamed first movement, mm. 1–6. Each movement seems to describe different aspects of her father, and the work begins with a bold, *fortississimo* statement, passionately marked *con fuoco*. I have included three examples containing my analysis: the prominence structure that also shows grouping structure (Ex. 57), a gradient barcode (Ex. 58), and a tree diagram (Ex. 59). All examples follow the forthcoming discussion.

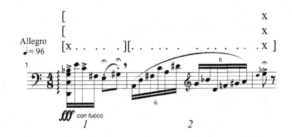

Example 57 León *Four Pieces for Solo Cello*, mm. 1–6: prominence structure

---

[18] Biographical information is taken from www.afm.org/2018/02/tania-leon-diversity-composing-life/.

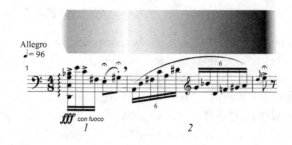

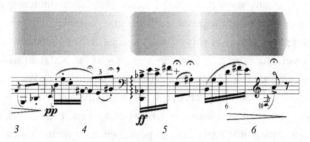

Example 58 León *Four Pieces for Solo Cello*, mm. 1–6: gradient barcode showing prominence structure

The grouping structure of this excerpt is less complicated because of an abundance of parallelism. At the lowest level, all boundaries are determined by proximity (GPR 2) because all groups end with a fermata and begin with a note without a fermata. As well, change (GPR 3) plays an important role because every group begins after a drop in register. The middle level presents a grouping issue: should it function as 3 groups + 2 groups or as 2+3? I have chosen 3+2 as a stronger reading of the groups because both resulting groups have a parallel construction (GPR 5), beginning at a loud dynamic with a rolled chord, and ending with a *decrescendo*. The listener might initially believe that the E-G# at the end of m. 4 parallels the E-G# in the first measure, but the octave is higher, and the following measure contains the pitches in the original octave. The boundary is somewhat ambiguous, lending the music a sense of unity and uninterrupted flow. This entire excerpt groups together, indicated by the subsequent measures.

In the prominence structure, several rules conflict. At the lowest level, both rolled chords are prominent due to their being at the low end of the pitch contour (PPR 1) and having loud dynamics (PPR 3). The E and A in mm. 3 and 6, respectively, occur at the high end of the pitch contour, and the F# has a long relative duration (PPR 2). Although the G has a fermata and is higher in pitch,

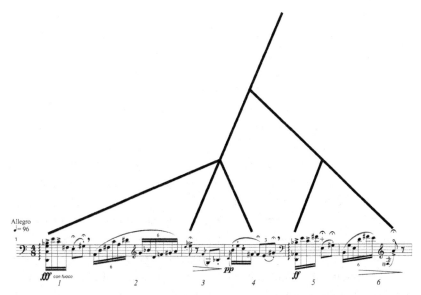

Example 59 León *Four Pieces for Solo Cello*, mm. 1–6: prominence structure as tree

the E-G# figure does not contain prominence in either of its other presentations, favoring the F# for that group.

In the middle level, the rolled chords initially appear as prominent, but a deeper inspection suggests the highest note of each respective group, largely because of pitch contour but also because of a central idea of upward pitch movement leading to a higher note. Even the first chord would be played in a way that it sounded like three lower notes leading up to the Bb, and there are several other upward lines that lead to longer, more prominent notes throughout this excerpt. At the third level, I have indicated the E is most prominent because it is relatively louder and higher than the final A. Further, the pattern of loud followed by a *decrescendo* in the notated dynamics is reflected in this construction; the final note would present as being less prominent given the phrasing arcs of the groups at the middle level.

4.3 Anthony R. Green – *Scintillation II*

Composer, performer, and social justice artist Anthony R. Green (b. 1984) cites Hyla as one of his teachers, but he has developed an entirely unique voice.[19] As an artist and entrepreneur, Green comments on issues related to racial injustice,

---

[19] Biographical information is taken from www.anthonyrgreen.com/bio.

the contributions of targeted and/or minority groups, immigration, and more, and he co-founded Castle of our Skins, an organization dedicated to celebrating Black artistry through music. In his *Scintillation II* (2008) for viola and cello, Green gives the performers a degree of rhythmic freedom. He states in the performance note that the piece is inspired by the gestures related to striking and igniting a match. He aims for freedom in the performance, so my analytical system can be a tool to aid performers in crafting their interpretations. The piece has no bar lines, but my analysis targets p. 8, line 4, through p. 9 line 3. In this section, the viola plays an ostinato over which the cello plays the analyzed excerpt. I have only included the cello part in my analyses because the solo part is not intended to match the ostinato in rhythm or tempo. In the provided examples, I have added letters to the groups at the lowest level for ease of reference. Following the discussion, please find the prominence structure (Ex. 60), gradient barcode (Ex. 61), and tree diagram (Ex. 62).

Grouping structure is uniformly delineated by proximity (GPR 2) at the lowest level. These gestures appear in three types: a pair of long notes with possible shorter embellishments (*A*, *B*, and *G*), downward contour within a decrescendo (*D*, *F*, *I*, and *J*), and upward contour within a crescendo (*E* and *H*). Even though group *C* contains a crescendo throughout, the pitch contour dips before jumping much higher and subsequently rising; this might suggest that group *C* should actually be divided into two groups at the change of register and contour direction, but very

Example 60 Green *Scintillation II*, p. 8 line 4, to p. 9 line 3, cello: prominence structure

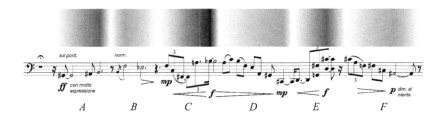

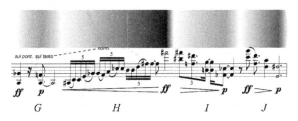

Example 61 Green *Scintillation II*, p. 8 line 4, to p. 9 line 3, cello: gradient barcode showing prominence structure

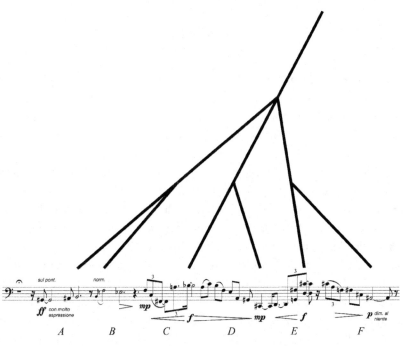

Example 62 Green *Scintillation II*, p. 8 line 4, to p. 9 line 3, cello: prominence structure as tree

Example 62 (cont.)

small groups are less preferable (GPR 1), and the overall energetic shaping of the gesture matches that of the others within a crescendo. Groups *A* and *B* are also small, but the length of the notes results in both gestures lasting the same duration or longer than the other gestures in this excerpt. As well, the change of timbre from *sul ponticello* to *normale* suggests there must be a grouping boundary between groups *A* and *B*. One could apply the same logic to group *G*, dividing it into two groups given the timbre and dynamic change, but the note values are shorter and would result in two groups of single notes that are much shorter in duration than the others in this excerpt. As such, group *G* remains intact. At the middle level, proximity is the justification for the boundary between *B/C*, *D/E*, and *F/G*. According to proximity, there might be a boundary between *H* and *I*, but *I* and *J* shows the same proximity as well as a change in register and dynamic. Symmetry would favor a boundary between *H* and *I*, but I have determined that change is a much more salient factor in my analytical framework. Further, parallelism shows that boundaries occur at the low end of the pitch and dynamic contour throughout the middle level. At the highest level, group *G* is parallel in structure to groups *A/B*, combined with the large proximity between attack points and drastic dynamic change.

Similar to grouping structure, the prominence structure is largely reliant upon duration (PPR 2) as the most salient factor. At the lowest level, events with the longest duration receive prominence in groups *A*, *C*, *D*, *F*, *G*, *H*, *I*, and *J*. In group *B*, the higher pitch (PPR 1) and the change (PPR 5) of timbre from *sul ponticello* to *normale* signal prominence on the F even though the Eb has a longer duration. In group *E*, parallelism suggests that the event at the top of the crescendo receives prominence, and the C# also has the highest pitch in the group. This is the pattern of prominence in the middle level, defining the structure for groups *C/D*, *E/F*, and *G/H/I*. In group *A/B*, the F would appear to be more prominent due to its higher pitch than the B, but such a structure would cause a clash with the following prominent Bb. As such, prominence would move away from the clash to the B, as indicated. At the highest level, duration and pitch contour combine to indicate prominence on the Bb and C#.

Green acknowledges the importance of gesture in his program note accompanying the score, so an understanding of energetic shaping throughout each phrase is paramount. His indicated hairpin dynamics lead to the longest and highest notes throughout, reinforcing the prominence indicated by duration and pitch. The sudden timbral and dynamic changes that are important to delineating structure reflect the dramatic inspiration of fire imagery.

4.4 Toru Takemitsu – *Orion*

Japanese Toru Takemitsu (1930–1996) was largely self-taught and combined elements of Eastern and Western music in his compositions. *Orion* (1984) is his only work written for cello and piano, and it comes from his *Orion and Pleiades* (1984) for cello and orchestra, one of several works about constellations.[20] Regarding temporality in the piece, Takemitsu stated, "Whereas the modern Western concept of time is linear in nature, that is, its continuance always maintains the same state, in Japan time is perceived as a circulating and repeating entity." The piece is constructed around repeating gestures over which the cello plays a melody, but the gestures are slow and contain enough space to avoid any perceived sense of repetition. My analysis targets a brief excerpt in which the cello plays alone, again highlighting an appropriate use of my analytical system to target an area without an even perceptual meter within a work that contains other sections with a clear sense of meter.

My analysis examines mm. 57–61. Temporal features that makes this excerpt a good candidate for analysis are the *freely* and *stretto* markings and the changing time signatures. I include this small fragment of music in order to show how my analytical system can be used to target a single specific phrase or short interjection of music that lacks a perceptible even beat. Very few pieces lack isochronous meter altogether, and

---

[20] Information is taken from www.allmusic.com/composition/orion-pleiades-for-cello-orchestra-mc0002473881.

my analyses are not meant to cover an entire piece, but rather to serve as a tool to clarify phrasing within certain sections of a larger piece. Following the discussion, please find the prominence structure (Ex. 63), gradient barcode (Ex. 64), and tree diagram (Ex. 65).

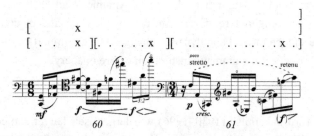

Example 63 Takemitsu *Orion*, mm. 57–61, cello: prominence structure

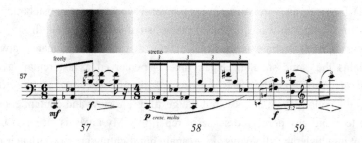

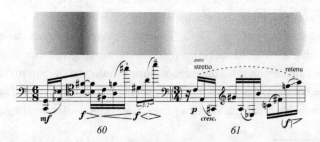

Example 64 Takemitsu *Orion*, mm. 57–61, cello: gradient barcode showing prominence structure

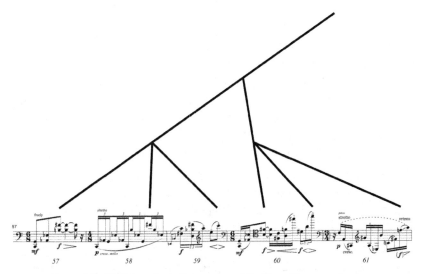

Example 65 Takemitsu *Orion*, mm. 57–61, cello: prominence
structure as tree

Most grouping boundaries occur as a result of proximity (GPR 2), although change and parallelism are also salient. At the lowest level, m. 59 displays a change to different rhythmic values after a measure of all triplet sixteenth notes (GPR 3). The first three events of m. 60 parallel the first group in m. 57, with an identical dynamic layout, suggesting that m. 60 divides into two groups. This parallelism suggests the boundary extends to the middle level, further strengthened by the sense of holding back at the end of both larger groups; the rhythmic values in mm. 58–59 gradually lengthen, and the end of m. 61 contains a *retenu*, although brief. The rests following this excerpt reinforce that this groups together at the highest level present.

The hierarchy of prominence is more complicated. At the lowest level, pitch contour (PPR 1) denotes stress in mm. 57–60. Measure 59 does contain a large change in the middle, shifting in register and timbre to the harmonic A (PPR 5), but the hairpin dynamic and the pitch height of the C override the changes. In the final group, it could be argued that the final note, A, would be more prominent due to its higher pitch and longer duration at the end of the *retenu*, but I believe that the indicated decrescendo is a suggestion from the composer to give prominence to the F instead. In the middle level, duration (PPR 2) is a primary factor, with the F#/B in m. 57 being significantly longer than any other event in the entire excerpt, and parallelism corresponding to m. 60. The extreme length of the initial F#/B in m. 57 suggests the event receives prominence at the highest level. As shown in the tree diagram, mm. 57–59 and 60–61 display very similar underlying structures, even though the pitches and rhythms vary widely.

5 Conclusion

When periodic even meter is present in music, two temporal structures exist: one emerging from the meter and the other from the musical surface. My analyses highlight the structure suggested by the surface in music that does not contain an even meter. In sections of music without perceptible meter, I argue that listeners perceive clear temporal constructions similarly to how they experience rhythm in language. My analytical framework, developed through the combination of GTTM and Hayes's stress theory from linguistics, addresses temporal structure based on perceptual prominence rather than perceptually salient meter. Although a rhythmic link has been identified between language and music, my research examines the concrete implications of such a connection, seeking to elucidate underlying musical structures as well as provide a tool for performers.

My mode of listening is based on gestural shapes, and I structure my analyses based on a hierarchy of events perceived as most salient within each gesture. Although this tool is applicable as high as the phrase level, broader relationships in a piece can be addressed through multiple points of local analysis. My analyses focus on temporality and rhythm and ultimately reveal motivic and pitch relationships that otherwise could be overlooked. One of the challenges in my work has been to balance and compare so many aspects of music as the patterns of prioritizations shift between each piece.

My analyses show the underlying temporal structure of six excerpts that are not structured with isochronous meter, and I compare the structures between two excerpts by Hyla to show how my method might address larger connections and patterns throughout a piece. Through an understanding of these structures, performers can approach a normative phrasing that will follow and enhance the listeners' experience of the music, showing temporal organization distinct from entrainment to meter. The unevenly spaced points of perceptual prominence inform the performer's approach to understanding form and phrasing. I present my analyses in three ways: prominence structure with brackets and /x/'s, gradient barcodes intended to show a map of phrasing for the performer, and prominence trees to compare different sections of music.

A listener's traditional sense of meter is based on the expectation of where beats will occur in time and a hierarchical relationship between them. In music without an even meter, the notated meter functions as an organizational tool for performers rather than a phenomenon experienced by the listener. As such, I suggest perceptual structures that operate in lieu of meter but still guide the music with a sense of expectation, tension, and energetic shaping. Within the pieces I have analyzed, there are sections with even periodic meter, but the purpose of this analytical tool is to examine the sections that operate under only one temporal structure. Through my analyses, I offer an alternative organization based on prominence and stress, suggesting order in situations that appear to be random.

References

Barlow, Harold, & Sam Morgenstern. *A Dictionary of Musical Themes*. 2nd ed. London: Faber & Faber, 1983.

Bigand, E., & Pineau, M. (1997). Global Context Effects on Musical Expectancy. *Perception and Psychophysics* 59, 1098–1107.

Chittum, D. (1971). Music Here and Now: Gesture and Organization in New Music. *American Music Teacher* 21(1), 23, 46.

Chomsky, N. (1957). *Syntactic Structures*, The Hague: Mouton.

(1965). *Aspects of the Theory of Syntax*, Cambridge, MA: MIT Press.

(1968). *Language and Mind*, New York: Harcourt Brace & World.

Daniele, J., & Patel, A. (2013). An Empirical Study of Historical Patterns in Musical Rhythm: Analysis of German & Italian Classical Music Using the nPVI Equation. *Music Perception* 31(1), 10–18.

Deliège, I. (1987). Grouping Conditions in Listening to Music: An Approach to Lerdahl & Jackendoff's Grouping Preference Rules. *Music Perception* 4 (4), 325–359.

Frankland, B., McAdams S., & Cohen A. (2004). Parsing of Melody: Quantification and Testing of the Local Grouping Rules of Lerdahl and Jackendoff's A Generative Theory of Tonal Music. *Music Perception* 21(4), 499–543.

Fry, D. (1955). Duration and Intensity as Physical Correlates of Linguistic Stress. *Journal of the Acoustical Society of America* 35, 765–769.

(1958). Experiments in the Perception of Stress. *Language and Speech* 1, 126–152.

Gibson, J. J. (1966). *The Senses Considered as Perceptual Systems*, Boston, MA: Houghton Mifflin.

Godøy, R. I., & Leman, M. (2009). *Musical Gestures: Sound, Movement, and Meaning*, London: Routledge.

Green, A. R. (2008). *Scintillation II*, Boulder, CO: Self-published by Composer.

Halle, M., & Vergnaud, J. R. (1987). *An Essay on Stress*, Cambridge, MA: MIT Press.

Hatten, R. S. (2004). *Interpreting Musical Gestures, Topics, and Tropes: Mozart, Beethoven, Schubert*, Bloomington, IN: Indiana University Press.

(2010). Performance and Analysis – Or Synthesis: Theorizing Gesture, Topics, and Tropes in Chopin's F-Minor Ballade. *Indiana Theory Review* 28(1/2), 45–66.

Hayes, B. (1995). *Metrical Stress Theory*, Chicago, IL: University of Chicago Press.

Huron, D., & Ollen, J. (2003). Agogic Contrast in French and English Themes: Further Support for Patel and Daniele (2003). *Music Perception* 21(2), 267–271.

Hyla, L. (1987). *Dream of Innocent III*, New York: Carl Fischer.

Hyla, L. (2002). *Amnesia Redux*, New York: Carl Fischer.

Jackendoff, R. (2003). *Foundations of Language: Brain, Meaning, Grammar, Evolution*, New York: Oxford University Press.

Jackendoff, R., & Lerdahl, F. (1981). Generative Music Theory and Its Relation to Psychology. *Journal of Music Theory* 25(1), 45–90.

Koelsch, S., Rohrmeier M., Torrecuso R., & Jentschke S. (2013). Processing of Hierarchical Syntactic Structure in Music. *Proceedings of the National Academy of Sciences of the United States of America* 110(38), 15443–15448.

Krumhansl, C. (1995). Music Psychology and Music Theory: Problems and Prospects. *Music Theory Spectrum* 17(1), 53–80.

Lalitte, P., Bigand, E., Kantor-Martynuska, J., & Delbé, C. (2009). On Listening to Atonal Variants of Two Piano Sonatas by Beethoven. *Music Perception* 26(3), 223–234.

Large, E., & Palmer C. (2002). Perceiving Temporal Regularity in Music. *Cognitive Science* 26, 1–37.

León, T. (1983). *Four Pieces for Solo Cello*, New York: Peermusic.

Lerdahl, F. (1992). Cognitive Constraints on Compositional Systems. *Contemporary Music Review* 6(2), 97–121.

   (2001). The Sounds of Poetry Viewed as Music. In R. Zatorre & I. Peretz, eds., *The Biological Foundations of Music*, New York City, NY: New York Academy of Sciences, vol. 930, pp.337–354.

Lerdahl, F., & Jackendoff, R. (1983). *A Generative Theory of Tonal Music*, Cambridge, MA: MIT Press.

Lester, J. (1986). Notated and Heard Meter. *Perspectives of New Music* 24(2), 116–128.

Liberman, M., & Prince, A. (1977). On Stress and Linguistic Rhythm. *Linguistic Inquiry* 8, 249–336.

London, J. (2012). *Hearing in Time: Psychological Aspects of Musical Meter*, 2nd ed., New York: Oxford University Press.

McNeill, D. (2000). *Language and Gesture*, New York: Cambridge University Press.

Palmer, C., & Krumhansl C. (1987). Independent Temporal and Pitch Structures in Determination of Musical Phrases. *Journal of Experimental Psychology: Human Perception and Performance* 13, 116–126.

Palmer, C., & Krumhansl C. (1990). Mental Representations for Musical Meter. *Journal of Experimental Psychology: Human Perception and Performance* 16, 728–741.

Patel, A., & Daniele, J. (2003a). An Empirical Comparison of Rhythm in Language and Music. *Cognition* 87, B35–B45.

(2003b). Stress-Timed vs. Syllable-Timed Music? A Comment on Huron and Ollen (2003). *Music Perception* 21(2), 273–276.

Peretz, I., & Coltheart M. (2003). Modularity of Music Processing. *Nature Neuroscience* 6, 688–691.

Takemitsu, T. (1984). *Orion*, New York: Schott Music.

Takemitsu, T. (1984). *Orion and Pleiades*, Tokyo: Schott Music.

Trevarthen, C., Delafield-Butt, J., & Schögler, B. (2011). Psychobiology of Musical Gesture: Innate Rhythm, Harmony and Melody in Movements of Narration. In E. King & A. Gritten, eds., *New Perspectives on Music and Gesture*, Abingdon: Routledge, pp. 11–44.

Zbikowski, L. (2011). Musical Gesture and Musical Grammar: A Cognitive Approach. In E. King & A. Gritten, eds., *New Perspectives on Music and Gesture*, Abingdon: Routledge, pp. 83–98.

Cambridge Elements ≡

Music since 1945

Mervyn Cooke
University of Nottingham

Mervyn Cooke brings to the role of series editor an unusually broad range of expertise, having published widely in the fields of twentieth-century opera, concert and theatre music, jazz, and film music. He has edited and co-edited *Cambridge Companions to Britten, Jazz, Twentieth-Century Opera*, and *Film Music*. His other books include *Britten: War Requiem, Britten and the Far East, A History of Film Music, The Hollywood Film Music Reader, Pat Metheny: The ECM Years*, and two illustrated histories of jazz. He is currently co-editing (with Christopher R. Wilson) *The Oxford Handbook of Shakespeare and Music*.

About the Series
Elements in Music since 1945 is a highly stimulating collection of authoritative online essays that reflects the latest research into a wide range of musical topics of international significance since the Second World War. Individual Elements are organised into constantly evolving Clusters devoted to such topics as art music, jazz, music and image, stage and screen genres, music and media, music and place, immersive music, music and movement, music and politics, music and conflict, and music and society. The latest research questions in theory, criticism, musicology, composition and performance are also given cutting-edge and thought-provoking coverage. The digital-first format allows authors to respond rapidly to new research trends, with contributions being updated to reflect the latest thinking in their fields, and the essays are enhanced by the provision of an exciting range of online resources.

Cambridge Elements ≡

Music since 1945

Elements in the Series

Music Transforming Conflict
Ariana Phillips-Hutton

Herbert Eimert and the Darmstadt School: The Consolidation of the Avant-Garde
Max Erwin

Baroque Music in Post-War Cinema: Performance Practice and Musical Style
Donald Greig

A Semiotic Approach to Open Notations: Ambiguity as Opportunity
Tristan McKay

Film Music in Concert: The Pioneering Role of the Boston Pops Orchestra
Emilio Audissino

Theory of Prominence: Temporal Structure of Music Based on Linguistic Stress
Bryan Hayslett

A full series listing is available at: www.cambridge.org/em45

Printed in the United States
by Baker & Taylor Publisher Services